D1510165

"Lays out how a greedy nobody insinuated himself into the Republican establishment . . . timely, compact, competent, and contains all the key facts, figures, and dates."
—Charles Trueheart, Bloomberg

"Peter Stone played a vital role in uncovering one of the biggest stories in Washington, and with this book he skillfully takes the reader deep inside the world of money, influence, politics, and power in a gripping and illuminating narrative."
—Michael Kranish, author, *Flight from Monticello: Thomas Jefferson at War*

"Peter Stone's first-rate investigative reporting, done over several years, is a deftly handled take by an experienced Washington reporter. The thing that makes this book stand out is the incredible amount of original reporting that went into it. The tale is also well written and not overly hyped. It doesn't have to be. It is told in delicious, understated detail that could easily be turned into a movie script."
—Anne Colamosca, co-author of *The Great 401(k) Hoax*

ABOUT THE AUTHOR

Peter H. Stone was one of the first reporters on the Abramoff story and has been following it closely since it broke in 2004. Since 1992, he has been a staff correspondent for the *National Journal*. His work has appeared in a number of newspapers and magazines, including *The Washington Post* and *The New York Times*, as well as *The American Prospect*, *The Atlantic*, *Mother Jones*, and *The Paris Review*.

CASINO JACK AND THE UNITED STATES OF MONEY

SUPERLOBBYIST JACK ABRAMOFF AND THE BUYING OF WASHINGTON

PETER H. STONE

MELVILLE HOUSE
BROOKLYN, NY

To my father, Marc Stone

Casino Jack and the United States of Money
first published in hardcover as *Heist: Superlobbyist Jack Abramoff,*
His Republican Allies, and the Buying of Washington by Farrrar, Staus,
and Giroux Copyright © 2006, 2010 by Peter H. Stone

First Melville House Printing: April 2010

Melville House Publishing
145 Plymouth Street
Brooklyn, New York 11201
mhpbooks.com

ISBN: 978-1-933633-69-5

Library of Congress Control Number: 2010923401

Designed by Jonathan D. Lippincott

Peter H. Stone worked as a consultant for the documentary *Casino Jack and*
the United States of Money, but the book and the documentary are separate works.

Contents

Prologue

■

It was far from a pedestrian guilty plea in Washington and, for Republicans, it marked an ominous start for 2006, a big election year.

What captivated Washington and the national media—and sent shivers through parts of the Washington lobbying community, the conservative movement, the Congress and the Bush administration—was the sight of celebrity lobbyist Jack Abramoff who had famously strong ties and friendships with many powerful Republicans, striding into a courtroom to plead guilty to charges that he conspired to corrupt public officials, defrauded four casino-rich Indian tribes out of almost $25 million, and evaded almost $1.7 million in taxes.

For almost a decade, Abramoff, together with his associates and clients at two well-known Washington law and lobbying firms, had doled out millions of dollars in campaign checks that had endeared him to dozens of members of congress. Abramoff's cachet with many high-profile GOP politicos was further magnified because he reveled in taking members and Hill staffers on golfing junkets overseas, treating them to free meals at his downtown D.C. restaurant, and hosting parties for them in sports suites at Washington's football and basketball arenas.

So when Abramoff, dressed in a black fedora and trench coat that recalled the garb of mafia chieftains in some Hollywood movies, appeared in court to enter a guilty plea on the morning of January 3, many political figures—and other lobbyists who knew the super lobbyist—had good reason to feel high anxiety, given their longstanding financial and other ties to the fallen influence peddler.

Not surprisingly, television, radio, and print reporters swarmed all over the courthouse steps in the hopes of snapping a picture of Abramoff or getting a glimpse of the man whose lobbying larceny had been well chronicled in national media for almost two years. Married with five children and forty-seven years old at the time of his plea, Abramoff was sent in late 2006 to a minimum-security jail in Cumberland, Maryland, where he was slated to serve a four-year term. Significantly, as part of his plea deal, Abramoff agreed to cooperate with the widening corruption probe.

"Jack was the Typhoid Mary of public corruption," says Guy Singer, who served as the co–lead prosecutor on the case for about two years before leaving the fraud section at Justice to join the law firm Fulbright & Jaworski. "If you see Jack as the hub, you have multiple spokes shooting out from him, not all of them interrelated."

Little wonder, then, that by late 2009, the sprawling DOJ-led investigation had turned into the biggest influence-peddling probe of the last decade, with serious ramifications for the GOP, the conservative movement, and the lobbying business. Likewise, the dread that many politicos and lobbyists had been feeling about Abramoff's plea proved remarkably well founded: the corruption probe into Abramoff's vast influence peddling operation had racked up a total of seventeen convictions of lobbyists, staffers, Bush-administration officials, and one member of congress. Among the bigger political figures ensnared in the scandal were Rep. Bob Ney (R-Ohio) and Steven Griles, the number two at the Department of the Interior, who were sentenced, respectively, to jail terms of thirty and ten months. Further, David Safavian, the Bush White House's top procurement official, is slated to start a one-year jail term in 2010 after being convicted by a Washington jury of obstruction of justice and lying to federal officials about his dealings with Abramoff.

The political fallout for other once–high-flying GOP officials has been widespread. In April 2006, then House Majority Leader Tom DeLay (R-Tex.) stunned many analysts when he announced that he would be retiring from office mid-year, a move prompted in good measure by two plea deals by former top aides to the Texan, Tony Rudy and Michael Scanlon, both of whom went from his office to become lobbying associates of Abramoff. DeLay was long under scrutiny in the probe for his close ties to Abramoff: over several years, Abramoff and his clients treated DeLay to three overseas junkets, and the Texan had helped a few of Abramoff's clients with legislative favors. As of late 2009, no charges had been filed against DeLay, and it looked as though he had dodged the legal bullet.

Subsequently, in the 2006 elections, several members with strong ties to Abramoff, including Sen. Conrad Burns (R-Mont.) and Reps. Richard Pombo (R-Calif.) and J.D. Hayworth (R-Ariz.), were defeated in part because their opponents capitalized on their links to the notorious lobbyist; Burns was a particularly inviting target, since over the years he had received more campaign cash than any other member, almost $150,000, from Abramoff's lobbying team and their clients. Even before Abramoff's plea, the Montanan had tried to distance himself by saying publicly that he wished Abramoff had "never been born."

Abramoff's plea also had repercussions for segments of the

conservative movement and two of its highest-profile leaders, Ralph Reed and Grover Norquist, who had been close friends and allies of the lobbyist for almost a quarter-century. Reed, the former Christian Coalition leader turned corporate consultant and GOP strategist, was so thoroughly tarred by revelations that he had received some $6 million from Abramoff's Indian casino clients that he lost his first race for elective office in 2006 after holding an early lead in his campaign to be Georgia's lieutenant governor. Democrats, who made the Abramoff scandal central to a number of races during the 2006 campaign, also promised to clean up such abuses if they captured the House and Senate. After the Democrats regained the majority on election day, the next Congress moved quickly to enact a lobbying and ethics re-form package that addressed a few of the abuses that had sur-faced in the influence-peddling scandal.

What's more, the outsized influence of many lobbyists in Washington became part of both presidential campaigns in 2008, with Barack Obama adopting more critical stances than John McCain even though the Republican had spent two years leading a Senate-committee probe into how Abramoff and his associates had fleeced six Indian-owned casinos out of almost $82 million. Given Obama's heated attacks on lobbyist influence in Washington, it wasn't surprising that the new president moved quickly when he took office to institute a set of curbs that limited lobbyists' access to and participation in his adminis-tration; this prompted loud grumbling among many of the city's approximately 15,000 registered lobbyists.

All of this fallout might well have surprised Abramoff, who, when he appeared in court on January 3, 2006, looked downcast while speaking softly and apologetically about his misconduct before Judge Ellen Huvelle. "All of my remaining days, I will feel tremendous sadness and regret for my conduct and what I have done," he said. "I only hope I can merit forgiveness from the Almighty and from those I have wronged or caused to suffer."

The lobbyist's plea that day had followed quickly after another one in November 2005 by Scanlon, the former DeLay spokesman, who had been Abramoff's covert lobbying partner in his Indian casino work and was part of a joint scam to cheat the tribes. Scanlon, who pled guilty to conspiracy and fraud charges, also agreed to cooperate with the widening Justice investigation.

In a statement of facts attached to Abramoff's plea, the government sketched the dimensions of the corruption scams that Abramoff and Scanlon had concocted. The two partners in lobbying larceny had "offered and provided a stream of things of value to public officials in exchange for official acts and influence and agreements to provide official action and influence. These things of value included, but are not limited to, foreign and domestic travel, golf fees, frequent meals, entertainment, election support for candidates for government office, employment for relatives of officials, and campaign contributions."

Adding to his woes, on January 4, Abramoff pled guilty in Miami to separate charges of conspiracy and wire fraud. The second plea involved a fraudulent $23 million wire transfer that Abramoff and a business associate and old friend, Adam Kidan, used in 2000 as proof of their down payment to swindle $60 million from lenders for their short lived acquisition of the Florida-based SunCruz Casinos, a small fleet of casino gambling boats. In March 2006, Kidan, who in 2005 pled guilty to similar charges, and Abramoff were each sentenced by a federal judge in Florida to five years and ten months; in Abramoff's case that sentence was later altered to be served concurrently with his other four-year sentence.

Abramoff's back-to-back pleas followed an almost two-year-long probe by the Justice Department and the FBI that continued through 2009 and into 2010.

Of the twenty defendants convicted in the scandal, Ney, who chaired the powerful House Administration Committee and who pled guilty to fraud and conspiracy charges in October 2006, stood out for his robust, symbiotic, and corrupt ties to Abramoff. Ney earned the nickname "the mayor of Capitol Hill" because, as chair of the administration committee, which oversees lobbying, federal elections, and the operations of the House, he had considerable power to dispense perks.

Ney was one of Abramoff's closest allies on the Hill; he helped the lobbyist and his clients with several significant legislative favors and benefitted handsomely in return.

At the time of his plea, Ney was fifty-two and had served six terms in the House. His plea details how he performed several favors for Abramoff, including putting two statements in the Congressional Record in 2000 that facilitated the SunCruz acquisition and introducing a measure aimed at reopening an Indian casino that was an Abramoff client. In exchange, Ney received hundred of thousands of dollar's worth of goodies, including free meals at Abramoff's restaurant Signatures, a five-day luxury-golf junket to Scotland in August 2002, plus lavish vacations in the U.S., free tickets to sporting events, and campaign contributions.

Neil Volz, a former chief of staff to Ney who pled guilty earlier in 2006, recalls that Abramoff and the congressman had a very tight working relationship, which Volz witnessed up close on the Hill and later in 2002, when he became part of Abramoff's lobbying team. "It was a mutually beneficial relationship between Bob and Jack," Volz told me in one of about a dozen talks we had over a year's time. "Bob helped Jack make money, and Jack helped Bob gain power."

These ties were exploited regularly by Abramoff and his associates. "There was no doubt Bob wanted to climb the ladder of power in the House," said Volz. "If he could help our clients while Bob achieved his goals, it was a classic Washington win-win." To help Ney achieve his goals, "there was a concerted effort to court DeLay and those close to him, including Tony Rudy and Mike Scanlon."

Volz still vividly recalls the mystique that surrounded Abramoff at Signatures, where he could simultaneously be a showman, a power-broker, and a deal-maker—all of which made him attractive to many members. "It was Jack's restaurant, and when Bob was there he was treated like a king," Volz remembers.

Other members were seduced by Abramoff's mystique and money. "Jack was a brand, not just a person," Volz stresses. "Members of Congress wanted to be associated with him. Being in his inner circle meant something. There was cachet to it."

That cachet plainly attracted many other Washington politicos from Congress and the Bush administration who were enticed by all the free perks that Abramoff dispensed with abandon and bravado and that ultimately became fodder for federal investigators and prosecutors. In making their cases against Abramoff and several of his lobbying associates, federal investigators found a trove of Abramoff e-mails and other records that provided invaluable incriminating evidence against other Hill staffers, lobbyists, and members of the Bush administration.

But despite this wealth of e-mails and hundreds of hours of cooperation from Abramoff and several of his key associates, complex corruption cases like this one are notoriously difficult to prosecute and sometimes don't yield as many indictments as are initially expected. Both defense lawyers and former prosecutors point out that although the Abramoff lobbying operation might appear to have corrupted many more than ultimately were charged with crimes, having enough proof to make charges stick isn't easy. "In the case of Abramoff, what appears disgusting isn't always illegal," explains Guy Singer, the former prosecutor. "Homing in on what actually crosses the line to be illegal is very challenging. Likewise, homing in on what can be proved is arduous."

Nonetheless, it's undeniable that besides all the convictions Justice notched, the scandal's ongoing revelations turned a bright spotlight on the nation's booming lobbying industry, in which Abramoff had been so important a player for a decade, at a time when the influence business was growing exponentially and new tools—several of which Abramoff was one of the first to popularize—were becoming widely used.

Abramoff had built a powerful influence machine that stood out in Washington for its conservative ideological drive mixed with bravado and stealth. Notwithstanding all his excesses and patently illegal acts, Abramoff was also a forerunner and trend-setter in the lobbying world in other key respects. His climb to the highest ranks of Washington's influence business was fueled in good measure by his ability to raise big bucks for members at a time when fund-raising demands were soaring and lobbyists increasingly were becoming mega-money harvesters for members, their leadership PACS, and party committees.

The influence network that Abramoff built with these tools was largely used to win favors for a motley mix of very high-paying clients, who often lacked experience in Washington: casino-owning Indian tribes, sweatshop owners in the far off Commonwealth of the Northern Marianas Islands, shady Russian energy moguls, and others with big tax, legislative, and regulatory needs in Washington.

Abramoff, whose years as a lobbyist were distinguished by his manic drive and vast ambition, seemed to remain very proud of his work despite the contrition that he exhibited when he appeared in court on January 3. Within weeks of his plea, he told a *Vanity Fair* writer that notwithstanding his mistakes—which he attributed largely to his style of operating at breakneck speed— "I was the best thing [the Indians] had going." Elsewhere in the interview and in other statements, Abramoff vacillated between feelings of guilt and boasting about his powerful GOP friends and numerous lobbying accomplishments. Feeling scorned by his longtime high-powered friends in Congress and the White House—including many members who rushed to return his campaign contributions and even President Bush, who had been photographed with Abramoff several times, the lobbyist quipped that "you're really no one in this town, unless you haven't met me."

When Abramoff arrived on the lobbying scene just after the GOP had won control of Congress in 1994, the influence business was poised for a period of explosive growth—in terms of the number of registered lobbyists, the fees that they earned, and the inordinate amount of influence that K Street exerts on Congress and the executive on issues ranging from the environment to health care to financial services.

Lobbying interests became increasingly successful in winning major policy fights in Washington: K Street regularly helped Detroit fend off efforts to increase fuel efficiency standards that the auto industry repeatedly argued would be too costly and onerous; lobbyists were also pivotal players during the 1990s in working with Wall Street investment giants to tear down longstanding regulatory rules that kept banks, insurers, and securities firms separate from one another. Both these lobbying battles were multi-year efforts that in retrospect, with the pain of the worst recession in decades still palpable, appear short-term—if not pyrrhic—victories that have proved costly to the long-term health of Detroit, Wall Street, and the nation's broader economy. Once more in 2009, financial-service, energy, and health-care interests poured hundreds of millions into lobbying and advertising drives—and accelerated campaign contributions to members—to derail or weaken major reform bills that would affect all three sectors and that were designed, to varying degrees, to expand regulation and oversight, curb longstanding abuses, and improve their overall financial health. One telling sign of how much money is now going to lobbying, and its rising influence in Washington, is that in 2009 some seventy former members of congress were registered to lobby just on financial service issues for an array of banks, hedge funds, insurers, and other financial interests.

Plainly, as spending on lobbying mushroomed in the 1990s and in the next decade—by 2009 it was well over a $3-billion-per-year industry—many lobbyists have exploited the power of campaign cash with a mix of gusto and guile akin to Abramoff's.

Rep. Dana Rohrabacher (R-Calif.), who might have been Abramoff's closest friend in Congress, candidly comments about the growing clout of the Washington lobbying world in Alex Gibney's documentary *Casino Jack*. "People should pay more attention to the fact that we have some enormous special interests in this country who are having dramatic influence on policy making," Rohrabacher told Gibney.

Abramoff's decade in the lobbying world exemplified in a particularly stark and ugly fashion the growing influence that lobbyists have in Washington policymaking. Abramoff's rise and fall is partly a tale of greed and ideological zealotry gone wild. It's also a tale of political corruption that the lobbyist spawned through an extremely powerful influence machine that his clients bankrolled. Ultimately, the scandal has shed new light on the often-toxic mix of money and politics: the corruption schemes that Abramoff fostered highlight the insidious ways that campaign cash and lobbying favors exert influence over decision-making in Washington.

ONE

Double-Dealing

■

When Jack Abramoff flew into El Paso in February 2002, he was greeted by the Tigua Indians as a potential savior. At least that's how Carlos Hisa, a soft-spoken and boyish-looking leader of the Tigua tribe, initially regarded the well-connected Republican lobbyist from Washington.

It was a difficult time for Hisa, the tribe's lieutenant governor, and other leaders of the thirteen-hundred-member Tiguas, a Native American Indian tribe who have been in the El Paso area since 1680. The tribe's fortunes had taken a big hit just days before Abramoff's arrival, when a federal court ordered that a highly profitable casino that the Tiguas had been running since 1993 be shuttered.

A lobbyist renowned for his prodigious fund-raising talents and high-level GOP contacts on Capitol Hill and with the Bush administration, Abramoff arrived at the Tiguas' headquarters with a pitch to help get their casino reopened that was hard to resist.

Hisa and other tribal leaders, who had worked hard for

months to stave off the casino's closing, were naturally interested, since the casino was vital to the tribe's welfare and employment.

At its peak, Speaking Rock Casino employed about eleven hundred people and generated almost $60 million a year in revenue, making it the economic mainstay for the small Tigua community. Most nights of the week and on weekends, the casino did a brisk business and was packed with patrons who poured in from nearby El Paso and other smaller towns to play the thirteen hundred slot machines or table games such as poker and blackjack.

Surrounded by palm trees, the adobe-style light brown Speaking Rock was more than just a profitable venture: a large chunk of the revenues from the one-story casino was channeled into badly needed health, education, and housing programs. One ambitious project that the casino largely underwrote was a $20 million state-of-the-art wellness center: it offered everything from a diabetes prevention and treatment program to karate classes for children to a modern Olympic-size swimming pool and other recreational facilities.

During the years the casino was operating, the tribe's unemployment rate, which had previously hovered around 50 percent, was close to zero. The casino also enabled the tribe some years to pay each tribal member between $8,000 and $15,000, and made possible health insurance for many Indians who would otherwise have received little or no medical care. In short, Speaking Rock had been an economic boon to the long-struggling tribe. Most of the tribe lives in a checkerboard-style development on some four hundred acres of land just a mile or two from the Mexican border and about half an hour's drive from downtown El Paso.

After researching the lobbyist's background, Hisa and other

tribal leaders were impressed. Abramoff's résumé read like a who's who of the GOP power elite. At the time, he was one of the hottest lobbyists in Washington and had received extensive and favorable press coverage. An Orthodox Jew and onetime Hollywood filmmaker who turned to lobbying right after the GOP captured Congress in 1994 during the Clinton administration, Abramoff had been lionized in front-page stories in *The Wall Street Journal* and *The New York Times*. The articles had detailed his herculean fund-raising work for GOP leaders such as Tom DeLay of Texas, who had once helpfully referred to Abramoff as "one of my closest and dearest friends."

Abramoff's roots in the conservative movement were deep. He counted among his oldest and closest friends two pillars of the network: Grover Norquist and Ralph Reed. Both men were confidants of Karl Rove, the Bush administration's political guru, and had been close allies of the lobbyist since the early 1980s, when Abramoff chaired College Republicans and they served successively as his chief lieutenants. Hisa was also impressed that Abramoff worked at Greenberg Traurig, an elite law and lobbying firm, one of whose Florida-based lawyers had been instrumental in helping the Bush campaign in 2000 win its legal battles in the Sunshine State.

A stocky, well-built man in his early forties who had once been a star weight lifter at Beverly Hills High School, Abramoff initially promised that he would do pro bono work. The lobbyist had a smooth, polished style about him, and he informed the Tiguas that their casino's closing was outrageous; in one e-mail to a tribal consultant he referred to the "gross indignity perpetuated by the Texas state authorities." Further, Abramoff boasted that he had already found some members of Congress who would correct the injustice, citing "a couple of senators willing to ram this through."

But to achieve that goal for the tribe, Abramoff urged the tribe to hire Michael Scanlon, former spokesman for DeLay turned public relations and grassroots consultant, whom he had introduced to the tribal council at a meeting on February 12. The lobbyist and his PR associate had flown into El Paso on a privately chartered Gulfstream II jet. Abramoff and Scanlon came to the meeting with the Tiguas sharply dressed: both wore dark pin-striped suits. A lanky, athletic man of about thirty with a reputation as a glib and fast-talking salesman, Scanlon received rave reviews from Abramoff: Scanlon was touted by the lobbyist as a "go-to guy" and the "preeminent expert in grassroots politics," whose expertise would quickly ratchet up local pressures on Congress to ensure that Speaking Rock would reopen. Moreover, Abramoff assured the council that they would be "hiring Scanlon independently." Unlike Abramoff's pledge to work for free, Scanlon readily acknowledged that his work would be expensive, and a few days later he followed up with a written plan that he felicitously dubbed "Operation Open Doors."

The Scanlon plan certainly sounded grandiose. "Operation Open Doors is a massive undertaking fueled by a nationwide political operation," the several-page plan stated. "This political operation will result in a majority of both federal chambers either becoming close friends of the tribe, or fearing the tribe in a very short period of time. The network we are building for you will give you the political clout you need to end around [sic] the obstacles you face in your own back yard. Simply put, you need 218 friends in the U.S. House and 51 Senators on your side very quickly, and we will do that through both love and fear." To achieve these objectives, Scanlon proposed several steps, including building a "grassroots data base" and a related "research data base" that his consulting company would assemble by compiling a master list of the tribe's vendors, employees, and other economic and political allies. "To put things in military terms," the Scanlon memo stated, "the grassroots data base is your weapon; and the research data base is your ammunition."

On February 22, when Hisa and the tribal council met to seal the deal with Abramoff, he was alone. As before, Abramoff stressed that there was a need for absolute secrecy about the project, which the lobbyist said was preferred by "friendly legislators" in Washington. "I thought Abramoff was for real," Hisa told me one day in the summer of 2005 as we sat in his modest office just across the street from where the Speaking Rock still stands. "I looked him up on the Internet. I had no reason to doubt him." It all sounded very good to Hisa and his colleagues on the Tigua council. So the tribe agreed to a $4.2 million contract with a Scanlon-run consulting company to launch Operation Open Doors.

At the outset, Hisa and the other tribal leaders had reason to be optimistic about their casino reopening. Marc Schwartz, an El Paso consultant for the tribe who was the main liaison with Abramoff, told me that even before the contract was signed, the lobbyist at the February 22 meeting had handed him a list of $300,000 in suggested donations that he wanted made quickly to dozens of members of Congress and campaign committees. Abramoff requested that the checks, more than 90 percent of which were for Republicans, be sent to him for distribution, which the tribe agreed to do. Schwartz recalled that he was a bit perplexed about Abramoff's repeated emphasis on secrecy but, like Hisa and the tribal leaders, thought that the lobbyist was a good find.

On March 20, Abramoff already had some good news: he informed the tribe's leaders that he had gotten a commitment from a little-known but influential House Republican, Bob Ney of Ohio, chairman of the House Administration Committee, to attach a measure in conference to an election reform bill that would permit the tribe's casino to reopen. Privately, after

Abramoff learned of Ney's promise at a meeting with the congressman, he couldn't contain himself. In a quick e-mail to Scanlon, he wrote, "We're fuck'n . . . gold. Ney is going to do Tigua."

Just six days after Ney's promise, Abramoff instructed the tribe to donate some $32,000 to Ney's campaign committee and newly created political action committee, which the Tiguas quickly did. For good measure, Abramoff asked the Tiguas to chip in $50,000 to help underwrite a golf junket to Scotland for Ney and two of his staff that August. In an e-mail to Schwartz, Abramoff alluded to Ney as "our friend" and strongly suggested that funding the trip would make the congressman happy. Despite the lobbyist's pressure, the tribe's council balked at the cost and Abramoff didn't hide his displeasure.

Not to be denied, Abramoff continued to press the tribe in e-mails and phone calls for help. Hisa recalled that Abramoff kept stressing how important the trip would be by pointing out that "he was going to take key individuals who we needed for our efforts." At one point, according to a Tigua consultant, Abramoff even went so far as to tell him that then House majority whip Tom DeLay, who had taken a similar golf trip to Scotland with Abramoff in 2000, endorsed the idea of Ney's taking a junket too.

Eventually, the Tiguas informed Abramoff that while they couldn't give their own funds, they would try to locate other financing. Hisa and Schwartz agreed to ask another small Texas tribe, the Alabama-Coushattas, which also might have benefited from the proposed legislation because they too had a casino project that was in jeopardy. Hisa met with a top official of the other tribe and explained that "we need $50,000 for a trip to Scotland for key individuals including Bob Ney." Shortly thereafter, the Alabama-Coushattas were instructed to send $50,000 to an obscure Abramoff-run charity in Washington called the

Capital Athletic Foundation. Abramoff had designated the foundation to sponsor and pay for the trip, which Abramoff billed as "an educational mission," to avoid public disclosure about its actual funding sources.

The summer getaway turned into an extravagant excursion that featured golf at Scotland's storied St. Andrews links, where Abramoff had hosted a similar junket for DeLay in 2000 and liked to entertain his powerful friends. The five-day trip, which cost about $130,000, wound up including a few people Abramoff was seeking political help from, as well as others with whom he already had close links. Besides Abramoff and Ney, there was Ralph Reed; Ney's former chief of staff Neil Volz, who in early 2002 had become a lobbying associate of Abramoff; and David Safavian, an old friend of Abramoff's in the Bush administration whom he had recently lobbied for other favors in Washington. The entourage flew to St. Andrews on a rented Gulfstream II jet and in Scotland enjoyed spacious $400-a-night rooms at the Old Course Hotel and some elegant dining in Edinburgh. There was also a two-day stopover at the expensive Mandarin Oriental Hyde Park Hotel in London on the way home. On House travel disclosure forms, Ney described the purpose of the junket as a meeting with Scottish parliamentarians, although Parliament was in recess during his visit. But Mark Tuohey, an attorney for Ney, told reporters shortly after Volz's plea deal that the congressman had been at a luncheon where there was a "discussion of issues" with a few Scottish parliamentarians. Tuohey declined to name the Scottish officials.

Just days after the junket in mid-August, Hisa, Schwartz, and one other Tigua representative came to Washington, where they met with Ney and Abramoff in the congressman's office for almost ninety minutes and received reassurances of his support for their cause. Hisa and Schwartz both recalled that Ney was in a spirited mood, praising the lobbying skills of Abramoff. "Ney thanked us for everything that the tribe had done for him," Hisa told me; but the congressman, who looked "red as a lobster" from his golf outing, didn't mention the trip specifically. Before the meeting, Abramoff had cautioned the tribal members that they shouldn't bring up the topic. He stressed that Ney would show his appreciation later, a not-so-subtle reference to the proposed legislation. According to his plea agreement, Volz was instructed by his new boss to tell Ney "what Abramoff wanted him to say."

Abramoff kept trying to impress the tribe with his Washington clout, Hisa told me. "Abramoff said that President Bush had contacted him and asked him to help find individuals to place in certain offices." Abramoff, Hisa added, also took credit for "recommending" Gale Norton to be secretary of the Interior Department, which oversees Indian issues.

Unfortunately for the Tiguas, the measure that Ney had told the tribe he would push for them never materialized, despite his pledge. Subsequently, Ney claimed that Abramoff had "misled" him about the proposed provision: the congressman said he had agreed to sponsor a measure only after Abramoff had told him that Democratic senator Christopher Dodd of Connecticut would also back the provision. Dodd denied he'd ever made such a commitment, but Ney cited his lack of support as the reason he backed out.

But in October of 2002, even after the election reform bill had been finished by the congressional conference committee without the measure to help the tribe, Ney told Tiguas officials in a conference call that he supported their efforts, according to Hisa and Schwartz. Ney also voiced dismay that Dodd, who cochaired the conference committee with Ney, "had gone back on his word," Schwartz told me.

The dashing of the Tiguas' expectations was just the start of the tribe's ordeal with Abramoff. Almost two years later, the tribe and Hisa were to learn other disturbing and depressing news: Abramoff and Scanlon had deceived them about their financial ties with one another and much more. Despite the lobbyist's pledge that he would initially work pro bono for the tribe, Abramoff had a secret deal with Scanlon to split most of the $4.2 million in fees that the PR man was receiving from the Tiguas. Abramoff and Scanlon each pocketed $1.85 million, according to their pleas.

And in an even more stunning revelation, Hisa and the tribe subsequently discovered that Abramoff and Scanlon, before they approached the Tiguas, had actually been engaged in a lobbying drive whose aim was to shut down the very same Speaking Rock casino they were now pressing to get reopened. Abramoff and Scanlon's covert work to shut the Speaking Rock was financed by another casino-owning tribe: the Louisiana Coushattas. Although the Tiguas were located almost eight hundred miles away, Abramoff had convinced the Louisiana Coushattas that both the Tiguas and the Alabama-Coushattas who were nearer the Louisiana border posed serious threats to their revenues. The lobbyist then enlisted Ralph Reed and his Atlanta consulting firm, Century Strategies, to generate conservative support from his old friends on the religious right for a lawsuit that had been filed by then Texas attorney general John Cornyn to shut down the Tiguas' casino on the grounds that it was in violation of state law. Reed worked in tandem with Abramoff and Scanlon, to rally Texas pastors and generate phone calls to bolster Cornyn's lawsuit.

In a January 2002 e-mail, Reed informed Abramoff that he was going to be meeting soon with one of Cornyn's top deputies, and added that "we did get our pastors riled up last week, calling his office . . ." Abramoff responded quickly: "Great. Thanks

Ralph. We should continue to pile on until the place is shuttered."

A few months earlier, in the fall of 2001, after the Tiguas took out large newspaper ads in Texas attacking Cornyn for using a "legal technicality" to close their casino and portraying the move as a blow to the Tiguas' economy, Reed e-mailed Abramoff: "Wow. These guys are really playing hardball. Do you know who their consultants are?" Abramoff shot back: "Some stupid lobbyists up here who do Indian issues. We'll find out and make sure all our friends crush them like bugs."

For Abramoff and his clients, Reed's enormous cachet with religious groups was enhanced by a *Time* magazine cover in May 1995 that featured his choir-boy visage and the headline "The Right Hand of God." But to judge by his own description of his electoral tactics during his years as executive director of the Christian Coalition, Reed was well versed in playing hardball. "I want to be invisible," Reed once told a Virginia newspaper in explaining his approach to mobilizing Christians for electoral purposes when he was spearheading the Christian Coalition for much of the 1990s. "I do guerrilla warfare. I paint my face and travel at night. You don't know it's over until you're in a body bag. You don't know until election night."

Reed's Texas mission was similar to projects he'd worked on with the two influence merchants in Alabama and in Louisiana. His forte in his new role as corporate consultant was mobilizing social and religious critics of gambling, many of whom he knew from his Christian Coalition work, to oppose tribal casinos and other gaming ventures that might pose economic threats to Abramoff's Indian clients. Together, these Abramoff-backed projects earned Reed's firm almost $6 million, but the funds were routed through a few conduits to protect Reed's image with his fellow Christian conservatives as an ardent foe of all gambling. For many months afterward, Reed staunchly maintained that Abramoff had simply asked him to build antigambling coalitions and that—even though he knew that the lobbyist had lucrative casino clients—he had no idea where his payments were coming from.

Hisa later read e-mails between Abramoff, Reed, and Scanlon that starkly revealed the lobbyist's playing both sides, as well as his cynicism. Just days before their casino was about to close, Abramoff had written to Reed that "I wish those moronic Tiguas were smarter in their political contributions. I'd love us to get our mitts on that moolah. Oh well stupid people get wiped out." To which Reed replied, "Got it." When the lobbyist and Scanlon were making plans for their visit to El Paso, he wrote to Scanlon, "Fire up the jet baby we're going to El Paso!!" Scanlon simply responded, "I want all their money." Abramoff assented, "Yawzah."

In another exchange that symbolized Abramoff's mind-set, the lobbyist dashed off an e-mail to Scanlon in which he gloated about some bad news for the tribe that ran in the *El Paso Times* on page 1. The story, which ran on Feburary 19, described the heavy economic toll that the casino's closing had on the tribe and pointed out that some four hundred and fifty casino employees were in the midst of being laid off. "Is life great or what!!!" Abramoff asked his colleague.

Hisa, a short man who wears his hair in a ponytail and sports a wispy goatee, told me that he's been haunted by the whole sordid episode. "I took a lot of the blame because I had pushed for the Washington effort," Hisa recalled with some pain but considerable candor. "I checked out Abramoff's credentials. Abramoff was educated in how to screw people over."

Hisa also voiced regrets about asking another tribe to make such a large donation to help Ney take his golf junket, especially since the legislation never came to pass. "I feel like I did what

Abramoff did to us." But what happened with the Washington lobbyist, he added, was "nothing new to the tribe." In Hisa's eyes, Abramoff's double-dealing and duplicity were part of a long story of mistreatment of Native Americans. "It's another chapter in an ongoing story."

That sense of history repeating itself is shared by several tribes that paid tens of millions of dollars to Abramoff and Scanlon for their lobbying, grassroots, and PR help. What happened to the Tiguas was actually just a fragment of a much wider pattern of frauds that Abramoff and Scanlon perpetrated on several Indian tribes flush with casino revenues.

The tribes that hired the two lobbyists were among the wealthiest in the country due to their casinos, which in some cases brought in $300 million or more annually. During the decade that Abramoff made millions of dollars and worked hard to keep GOP coffers brimming, the Indian gaming industry was also growing at a rapid pace: by the end of 2005, Indian casinos were a $20-billion-a-year business and represented the fastest-growing segment of the nation's gambling industry.

But despite their newfound wealth, some of the tribes lacked political savvy about Washington and the ways of the lobbying world. "I feel like we were taken advantage of by these white guys again," Audrey Falcon, a council member of the Saginaw Chippewa tribe in northern Michigan, told me one crisp fall morning in 2005 at the tribe's Soaring Eagle Casino and Resort complex in Mount Pleasant. "It brings up all the mistakes that we've had in our history."

Falcon, a former nurse, and mother of two, who speaks with conviction, thinks that the tribe's casino revenues made it a ripe target. "Abramoff and Scanlon knew that we had money and a successful gaming operation. We were targeted because of that, I sense." The Saginaw Chippewas spent almost $14 million to hire Scanlon's company, and Abramoff, and, like the Tiguas, had no knowledge that he had a secret kickback deal with Abramoff. "It's really sad that this kind of thing is happening again. Even though Abramoff is gone, we're still dealing with him and it's hurtful."

The bitter and very costly experiences that the Tiguas, the Saginaw Chippewas, and several other tribes had with Abramoff and Scanlon helped lift the lid on a giant influence-peddling scandal. Ultimately, it was revealed that six tribes paid Abramoff and Scanlon the extraordinary sum of $82 million over three years for their lobbying and PR help.

The outlines of the scandal began to emerge after *The Washington Post* ran a long front-page exposé on February 22, 2004, that revealed significant details about the extraordinarily high fees that the two men charged; in the story, several tribal leaders raised concerns about the lack of results and the skimpy documentation of expenditures. In the wake of the *Post* story, the Senate Indian Affairs Committee launched an extensive investigation into allegations by tribal leaders that they had been bilked out of millions of dollars. Almost simultaneously, a federal task force led by the Justice Department revved up a nascent criminal probe into similar allegations that the two men had hoodwinked the casino-rich tribes.

The Senate hearings uncovered a mountain of evidence—including a treasure trove of e-mail traffic among Abramoff, Scanlon, and other lobbying colleagues that detailed the often bizarre and complex cons they used to manipulate tribes into paying them humongous fees. Abramoff and Scanlon seemed to have insatiable appetites for more deals and more money. On December 7, 2002, Abramoff e-mailed Scanlon: "We really need mo money . . . We are missing the boat. There are a ton of potential opportunities out there. There are 27 tribes which make over $100 million a year . . . We need to get moving on them."

That hunger for money—for both personal and political

ends—explains much about the casino-lobbying heist: the Indian casinos were really giant piggybanks for the two men to enrich themselves and dozens of conservative GOP friends such as Reed and Norquist, who provided lobbying and other help in Washington and several states. Using a scheme that they dubbed "Gimme Five," the two men had persuaded six tribes to pay an astonishing total of $66 million over a three-year period from 2001 through 2003. The huge fees, which for some tribes rivaled what Fortune 500 companies spend yearly on their lobbying efforts in Washington, were paid to two of Scanlon's firms, which were hired at Abramoff's behest for their specialized services. The heart of the Gimme Five scam was surprisingly simple: unbeknownst to the tribes, Abramoff had cut a kickback deal with Scanlon to split most of the revenues between them, yielding them each almost $21 million in profits.

On top of the $66 million, the law and lobbying giant Greenberg Traurig, where Abramoff was a famed rainmaker, was paid $16 million over three years by the tribes. And the tribes, at Abramoff's urging, also doled out millions more to a variety of nonprofits, charities, conservative think tanks, and mostly GOP campaign coffers; Abramoff suggested that such actions would produce political benefits.

There was a good reason why Abramoff was fixated on signing up tribal casinos to build his lobbying practice. Indian casinos—which faced political battles regarding taxation, sovereignty, federal recognition, and competition—were expanding fast when Abramoff entered the lobbying business and were viewed as potential gold mines for hungry lobbyists. Historically, Indian gaming started to take off after 1988, the year that Congress passed the Indian Gaming Regulatory Act, which opened the doors wide for new Indian casinos. In the late 1980s and early 1990s, numerous tribes came to view casino gaming as an important avenue to promote economic growth.

For Abramoff, Indian casinos represented a jackpot that he exploited in stages. Early on in Abramoff's lobbying career in the mid-1990s, he won some big victories for his first client, the Mississippi Choctaws, but several years later he ripped them off when he had them hire Scanlon for extra help. When Abramoff and Scanlon joined forces in 2001, the financial scalpings began in earnest as the two men plotted with brazen abandon to get more business. After hearing from Scanlon that he'd just received a $3 million payment from the Louisiana Coushattas, Abramoff fired back: "You are a great partner. What I love about our partnership is that when one of us is down the other is always there. We're going to make dollars for years to come."

Spearheaded by Senator John McCain of Arizona, a longtime passionate critic of lobbying and campaign finance abuses, the Senate Indian Affairs Committee probe turned into a massive two-year inquiry into the financial and political machinations of Abramoff and Scanlon. At his first hearing in the fall of 2004, McCain pointed out that the still unfolding scandal was "astonishing" in sheer dollar terms. "Every kind of charlatan and every type of crook" has exploited American Indians since the sale of Manhattan island; McCain added that "what sets this tale apart, what makes it truly extraordinary, is the extent and degree of the apparent exploitation and deceit." At a later hearing in mid-2005, McCain observed that Abramoff and Scanlon's treatment of their clients constituted a "betrayal." At least equally if not more galling to the tribes' self-esteem were dozens of e-mails between the two men—and some of their colleagues—in which Abramoff and Scanlon referred to their tribal clients with contempt, calling them "troglodytes," "morons," "monkeys," and "imbeciles."

The enormous haul of Indian casino money that Abramoff and Scanlon raked in, coupled with serious allegations of misconduct, quickly attracted a few dozen federal investigators from the FBI and other agencies. Under the direction of a multi-agency task force led by the Public Integrity and Fraud units of the Justice Department, a separate criminal probe into Abramoff's influence peddling was by mid-2004 in full swing. Ultimately, the Justice plea agreements with Scanlon and Abramoff focused on fees paid by four of the six tribes that they jointly represented. Those four tribes—the Tiguas, the Saginaw Chippewas, the Louisiana Coushattas, and the Mississippi Choctaws—paid Scanlon's companies a total of $53 million, of which a little less than half was kicked back to Abramoff through their Gimme Five scheme.

Eventually that probe branched out into a broader public corruption investigation involving other lobbying and business projects of Abramoff, whose work encompassed both foreign and domestic clients, some of whom had unsavory and colorful histories. One of Abramoff's more bizarre and disastrous projects involved his brief and stormy acquisition of SunCruz Casinos, a fleet of gambling boats that was under scrutiny by a separate federal grand jury in Florida. Tragically, within months of the deal's closing in September 2000, things turned ugly. On February 6, 2001, Konstantinos "Gus" Boulis, the previous owner of SunCruz, was brutally murdered in a gangland-style hit in Fort Lauderdale; no one was charged until September of 2005, when three men were arrested, two of whom had been hired as catering and surveillance consultants by Abramoff's business associate, Adam Kidan.

While the SunCruz story reeked of *Miami Vice* and had a tabloidlike feel to it, Abramoff's lobbying career in Washington too had long generated gossip and plenty of publicity because of its larger-than-life dimensions and the lobbyist's stellar conservative pedigree. Abramoff, who had long commanded fees between $500 and $750 an hour and who was known by the moniker "Casino Jack," was a mass of paradoxes. A longtime movement conservative and Orthodox Jew, Abramoff in his e-mails and lobbying activities indulged in profanities, deceptions, and frauds. Although famed for his public fund-raising and wining and dining of members of Congress, Abramoff also was a stealthy operator who funneled millions of dollars through conduits and front groups to enrich himself and his political allies and chosen causes. Moreover, while he boasted many powerful friends in Congress and the Bush administration, Abramoff, in his drive to win business, exaggerated his influence and contacts and was a serial name-dropper. He was regarded by many friends as a generous and philanthropic soul, but he also had a distinctly greedy side.

In his drive to win political friends and legislative favors, Abramoff used high-profile venues to cozy up to the powerful. Abramoff controlled four luxury sports suites at Washington's leading football, basketball, and baseball stadiums that he rented for roughly $250,000 apiece, fees that were largely underwritten by his Indian casino and foreign clients. For extra cachet and clout, Abramoff became a restaurant entrepreneur: in February 2002 he opened Signatures, an upscale eatery located not far from Capitol Hill and the White House, which almost overnight became a popular hangout for members, staffers, and Bush administration friends, as well as a choice spot for holding GOP fund-raisers.

Historically, Abramoff's fortunes were closely linked to one of Washington's most powerful fund-raising machines that lobbyists have dubbed "DeLay Inc." Abramoff's ties with DeLay were cemented by hundreds of thousands in contributions that he raised from clients for the Texan's campaigns, political committees, and pet projects—including lavish foreign golf junkets, nonprofits, and charities. To further bolster his ties to DeLay, Abramoff hired three of his top aides as lobbying associates. Some of the aides had demonstrated their worth by giving

Abramoff excellent access when they worked in DeLay's office. Subsequently, after they became his lobbying colleagues, these ex-aides performed similar tasks for Abramoff's clients while earning $200,000 to $300,000 a year.

Yet Abramoff was too shrewd an operator to bank just on DeLay for access and influence. Over the years, Abramoff also adroitly recruited several senior aides from other such Republican members as Bob Ney, John Doolittle, and Conrad Burns, who were to prove important to his clients' lobbying successes. His lobbying associates were mostly men in their late twenties or early thirties who were drawn to Abramoff's flashy and high-rolling lifestyle. "They were young, most Catholic and aggressive guys who came from more modest backgrounds and wanted to overachieve," recalled one such former Abramoff associate who made the jump from the Hill to lobbying. To former colleagues of the disgraced lobbyist, Abramoff provided a kind of full-service concierge service for Capitol Hill friends and clients alike. As a former colleague of Abramoff's put it, the lobbyist liked to have people "owe him" so that he could call in his chits at the right moment. Likewise, his former colleagues tell stories about Abramoff's infatuation with the movie *The Godfather*, which became a regular source of office repartee between the lobbyist and his associates. "Jack was new to the scene," recalled John Feehery, a former aide to DeLay and House Speaker J. Dennis Hastert. "He was trying to make a big splash. He was very flamboyant . . . Not only was it over the top, but now it seems like it was over the line."

The story of how Abramoff ingratiated and allied himself with DeLay and other leaders in the GOP Congress is emblematic of the links forged between Republicans and K Street lobbyists after the capture of the House in 1994. Several veterans of the so-called GOP revolution view Abramoff's meteoric rise and fall—which helped precipitate DeLay's demise as House majority leader and tarred other GOP luminaries in and out of Congress—as ultimately a cautionary tale about the betrayal of principles and political corruption.

Paul Erickson, who like Reed and Norquist was a veteran of College Republicans and remained a good friend of Abramoff's, was dismayed to learn of Abramoff's secret deals with Scanlon. "The arrangement with Scanlon and the kickbacks were shocking to me," Erickson, who is now a South Dakota–based businessman, told me in a phone interview in mid-2005. "It was so unnecessary . . . It seemed like unbridled avarice." For many, Abramoff's rise and fall on K Street contains broader lessons about how the GOP in recent years chose to exercise control over the levers of power in Washington. "There was an environment created in Washington that allowed someone like Abramoff to rise to the heights he achieved," Marshall Wittmann, a onetime lobbyist for the Christian Coalition turned moderate Democrat, told me one afternoon in Washington. "The Republican Congress has become a bordello for big money. Abramoff is the one who got caught because he went too far."

While Democrats too exploited fund-raising and the lobbying community to their advantage when they were in power, Wittmann is not alone in his view that a period of excess followed the GOP takeover of Congress in 1994. And a number of observers point to the DeLay-and-Norquist-inspired K Street Project—with its focus on prodding companies, trade groups, and lobbying firms to hire more GOP lobbying muscle and raise more bucks—as exhibit number one to explain the changed environment. "There was always a close relationship between K Street and the Hill, but it became much more pronounced and disciplined when the Republicans took over," in Wittmann's judgment.

The Indian casino–lobbying game that Abramoff dominated for several years made him very attractive to members constantly searching for campaign cash. During most of the Clinton years, the bulk of tribal giving had gone to Democrats, and Republicans like DeLay were eager to reverse that trend. With Abramoff's constant prodding, several tribes expanded their giving to his GOP friends in Congress. At the zenith of his Indian casino–lobbying career, six tribes with casinos that Abramoff represented donated some $3.5 million in a three-year period between 2001 and 2003, of which some two-thirds went to GOP members and campaign committees.

Abramoff's drive, ambition, and self-image went far beyond lobbying. As the scandal unfolded, it became evident that Abramoff had served as a kind of financial godfather to a conservative influence machine. The beneficiaries ranged from Reed and Norquist to much more obscure conservative groups like the National Center for Public Policy Research and the Council of Republicans for Environmental Advocacy. Abramoff's enormous influence as a fund-raiser for GOP candidates and conservative causes made him a heroic figure to many on the right. One such friend and political comrade was Rabbi Daniel Lapin, who ran Toward Tradition, a nonprofit group designed to build ties between conservative Jews and Christians, of which Abramoff was an early supporter and board member. Not long after the scandal first broke, Lapin, who is said to have introduced Abramoff and DeLay, told me that the lobbyist was one of the "most creative, charismatic and driven people I've ever known."

Likewise Reed, soon after the scandal initially made headlines, told me that Abramoff was a "new and different kind of lobbyist," who is "more identified as a strategist and builder of the Republican majority than for his lobbying practice alone." Reed adamantly maintained for months that he had never worked for a casino, while trying to downplay his long-standing ties with Abramoff. But to Reed's embarrassment, Senate investigators discovered e-mails that contradicted his oft-repeated denials of any financial ties to gambling and underscored Reed's close links to Abramoff. "Hey, now that I'm done with the electoral politics, I need to start humping in corporate accounts! I'm counting on you to help me with some contacts," Reed wrote Abramoff in November 1998, just a year after he'd left his post at the Christian Coalition. Within months, Reed was earning money by doing work for the Mississippi Choctaws on anti-gambling projects in Alabama that Abramoff had arranged.

Similarly, Norquist, whose public persona is often that of a rumpled conservative firebrand, vigorously defended Abramoff's integrity. In the spring of 2004, Norquist seemed to blame much of the criticism of Abramoff on a political vendetta by McCain because he had not gotten the GOP presidential nomination in 2000. "The Senator," Norquist charged in an interview with me in 2004, "hates Bush and hates DeLay." But he quickly added, "Jack is an ally and friend of both." Norquist, who worked against McCain in the 2000 primaries, asserted further that Abramoff would weather the investigation and be "fine." He called Abramoff "hard-working, smart, and completely up-front."

Abramoff's defenders notwithstanding, several of the scams that he used to funnel tribal monies to conservative friends and his own bank accounts and pet projects had such a zany, madcap quality that it seemed as though they could have been lifted from Mel Brooks's *The Producers*. In one of the oddest twists, Abramoff persuaded a few tribal clients to donate almost $4 million—directly and indirectly—to his personal charity, the Capital Athletic Foundation. The charity touted its mission as helping poor kids in urban areas and promoting sportsmanship. But the lion's share of the foundation's funds went to the Eshkol Academy, a Jewish prep school that Abramoff had also founded in suburban Maryland, which two of his sons briefly attended.

Millions more were routed through a self-styled "international think tank" that was located in a small yellow bungalow in Rehoboth Beach, Delaware, a popular seaside getaway just a few hours from downtown Washington. Dubbed the American International Center, the think tank was the handiwork of Scanlon, who had created it with Abramoff's blessing to disguise where funds were coming from, where they were going, and what kind of work was being done for different tribal and foreign clients. A key mission of the think tank was to channel about $2.3 million of tribal funds to Ralph Reed's consulting company to help keep his involvement with Indian casinos secret, thereby allowing him to maintain his good standing with social and religious conservatives who since his Christian Coalition days had regarded him as a staunch foe of gambling. Adding to the center's mystique, Scanlon's two principal deputies were boyhood friends from the beach, one of whom was a yoga instructor and the other a lifeguard.

As appalling as the frauds and cons committed by Abramoff and Scanlon were, it would be naïve and unfair to let some of the tribal leaders who retained the two influence peddlers completely off the hook in terms of responsibility. "The thought of acquiring political power was a narcotic for some of these tribes," I was told by Kevin Gover, a Native American who was director of the Bureau of Indian Affairs during the Clinton administration and then taught law at Arizona State University. "They lost their minds and got ripped off."

Looking back at their very expensive and painful encounters with Abramoff and Scanlon, some tribal leaders also see cautionary lessons. No tribe probably felt as injured as the Louisiana Coushattas, who spent more than any other—at least $32 million—to hire the two Washington hands. "Abramoff and Scanlon had a talent for exploiting weaknesses," observed David Sickey, a very articulate man in his late twenties who was elected to the Coushatta council in mid-2003 and pushed to uncover the frauds and get rid of Abramoff and Scanlon. "It's a sad fact that they were looking to take advantage of Indian wealth," Sickey told me one morning in early 2006 when I visited the Coushattas' tribal offices. "They had a talent for sniffing out weak links. At the end of the day we learned some important and painful lessons."

That feeling was certainly shared by several other tribes, such as the Tiguas. Even after Ney failed to deliver on his promised measure to help the Tiguas reopen Speaking Rock, in 2003 Abramoff pitched more schemes to the tribe to win additional business from them. One of the most bizarre notions Abramoff suggested involved an insurance scam that the tribe quickly rejected. It's not hard to see why: in an e-mail to Tigua consultant Marc Schwartz, Abramoff tried to persuade the tribe to enroll tribal elders seventy-five and older in a term-life insurance program and make Eshkol Academy the beneficiary. The school would then pay Abramoff's lobbying fees, he said. Appallingly, too, the work that Scanlon, with Abramoff's blessing, had billed the Tiguas for was outrageously priced. Hisa of the Tiguas told the Indian Affairs Committee at a hearing in the fall of 2004 that Scanlon charged his tribe close to $1.5 million for the much-ballyhooed data base to mount Operation Open Doors, only to discover later that its true value was less than $100,000. It's not surprising that in his congressional testimony, Hisa quipped, "A rattlesnake will warn you before it strikes. We had no warning."

TWO

The Birth of a Lobbyist

■

On a winter afternoon in early 1995, the large conference room on the fifth floor of Preston Gates & Ellis, a well-established Seattle law firm with a small but growing Washington lobbying practice, was packed with veteran lawyers and new recruits. The occasion was special: Tom DeLay of Texas, a leader of the GOP revolution that had just captured control of the House of Representatives for the first time in four decades, was dropping by to attend a meet and greet that offered lobbyists a prized opportunity to chat informally and socialize with the man who had just assumed the job of House majority whip.

The get-together was the handiwork of the newest member of the firm's lobbying team, Jack Abramoff. Although he'd been working there for only a few weeks and lacked government experience, Abramoff had pulled off an impressive coup by getting the GOP's third-most-powerful man in the House to visit the firm. One participant that day recalled DeLay telling a story that underscored a favorite theme of the Republican who soon earned the nickname "The Hammer" for his aggressive fund-raising and House leadership style. DeLay's tale was really a simple political parable about the need to increase campaign contributions: it focused on a Texas company that wanted legislative help with a road project but couldn't get the necessary political backing because it hadn't contributed enough to legislators or done the right lobbying.

It was an auspicious beginning to Abramoff's lobbying career and impressed many of the older hands at the firm, one of whose name partners was Bill Gates, Sr., father of the Microsoft mogul. "It was a big deal," recalled a Preston Gates veteran who attended the meet and greet. "He was able to deliver DeLay very fast." In coming months and years, delivering DeLay was to become one of the hallmarks of Abramoff's lobbying successes for his clients.

Abramoff's cachet with the conservative GOP leadership was soon palpable, as he quickly signed up a few high-paying clients and began to deliver results. Within a few months, Abramoff snared his first Indian casino client, the Mississippi band of Choctaw Indians, a tribe that ran one of the most successful of the new breed of Indian casinos. The Choctaws were desperately trying to kill a tax measure that was championed by Representative Bill Archer of Texas, the powerful chairman of the House Ways and Means Committee whose jurisdiction includes tax issues. The Archer measure threatened the tribe with a levy on casino revenues and was pending in a conference committee in mid-1995 when Abramoff and the firm were retained at the last minute to stop it.

From the start, Abramoff had a knack for framing his lobbying efforts in language that echoed the conservative principles embraced by his allies. In the Choctaws' case, Abramoff's message stressed that the tribe's opposition to the Archer proposal deserved support from conservatives because it mirrored the GOP's broad commitment to blocking tax increases. The argument was pushed hard by Norquist and his powerful grassroots antitax behemoth, Americans for Tax Reform, and gained enough backing from DeLay and some other House leaders to give the Choctaws and Abramoff's team a quick victory and burnish Abramoff's lobbying credentials.

The win for the Choctaws, which saved the tribe many millions in taxes, was the first of several efforts over the years in which DeLay and Norquist figured as key political allies for Abramoff and his clients. At Abramoff's behest, the Choctaws soon became a sizable financial angel for DeLay's political operations as well as Norquist's organization. The Choctaws also helped to underwrite other projects that boosted Abramoff's power base in Washington: the tribe became annual sponsors of a charity golf tournament to benefit the DeLay Foundation for Kids and paid close to $250,000 a year to sponsor sports skyboxes in Washington that Abramoff used to wine and dine Capitol Hill friends.

The duo of DeLay and Norquist also provided an effective one-two punch in helping another of Abramoff's first clients, the Commonwealth of the Northern Mariana Islands (CNMI), repeatedly defeat Democratic proposals that would have imposed tougher labor regulations. The economy of the Marianas, a U.S. territory in the Pacific, depended heavily on its garment-manufacturing industry, which was under attack for paying workers $2 an hour less than the U.S. minimum wage.

Over the next six years, these two clients were to form the backbone of a hugely successful lobbying practice that Abramoff built and which, by the year 2000, put him near the top of GOP power brokers on K Street. Together the Choctaws and the Marianas paid close to $15 million during this period for Abramoff and his firm's services. Their lucrative business, along with a few of Abramoff's other clients—including Channel One and a Puerto Rican business coalition seeking statehood for the island—helped catapult Preston Gates from its midlevel rank among Washington lobbying firms into the top ten firms on K Street.

From the start of Abramoff's Preston Gates lobbying career, his style was distinctive. "None of us thought the way that Jack did," a former colleague remembered. "He tried to fit the model of conservative Republicans. He was a different animal from us. Jack thought in big-picture terms." Washington had been run by Democrats for many years, and Abramoff early on worked hard to "create an intellectual counterforce to received wisdom," he added. It was no accident that Abramoff's arrival at Preston Gates coincided with the GOP's capture of Congress and the advent of a conservative agenda that focused heavily on the slashing of regulations and big tax cuts, especially for the rich.

Washington's leading lobbying firms had tilted Democratic in the late 1980s and early 1990s. But the 1994 elections spurred many lobbying shops to search for and hire more Republicans to ensure that they had the right connections with the new GOP majority. The shift, which began almost immediately after the elections, was pushed hard by DeLay and Norquist through their aggressive drive to boost Republican hiring on K Street in order to transform the lobbying community both ideologically and financially.

DeLay, a onetime small-business man who ran Albo Pest Control, an exterminating company in the Houston area, had a particular animus for government regulations, an ideological passion that he shared with large segments of the business community and his fellow conservatives. Before his election to Congress in 1984, DeLay had served for six years in the Texas legislature, where he was nicknamed "Mr. DeReg." DeLay had an almost visceral hatred of government regulations, a dislike that had been fed by his own encounters with the Environmental Protection Agency, which he later likened to the Gestapo. Environmental curbs, such as pesticides rules, "drove me crazy," he has said. Little wonder that rolling back government regulations became a centerpiece of DeLay's agenda and that one of his first efforts as majority whip was working closely with dozens of lobbyists through a coalition called Project Relief to curb regulations.

The K Street Project was part old-fashioned spoils system for the victors combined with a new GOP thrust to bring in much more campaign loot from corporate America. In the wake of the 1994 elections, key House conservatives led by DeLay wanted to remake the lobbying world as fast as possible because it seemed to offer them the royal road to campaign riches. To do that, DeLay and other House heavyweights bluntly informed companies that if they wanted to get in to see GOP leaders, they had better have GOP lobbyists working for them. In one telling incident, described by reporters David Maraniss and Michael Weisskopf in their book *Tell Newt to Shut Up!* DeLay berated a top corporate executive for employing a "hard-core liberal" and warned the executive that in the future if he wanted access "you need to hire a Republican." The CEO took the message to heart and the liberal was sent to the firm's London office.

Norquist was equally direct in spreading the word about the goal. In a 2005 interview with Elizabeth Drew published in *The New York Review of Books*, he said, "We don't want nonideological people on K Street, we want conservative activist Republicans on K Street." Over the years, many CEOs took these messages to heart and responded quickly by bringing in more GOP blood from Capitol Hill and other places. "K Street was willing to pay huge amounts of money for access," Marshall Wittmann, the former Christian Coalition lobbyist, told me. "The revolving door between the Hill and K Street swung much more quickly with staffers going to K Street en masse for very lucrative jobs."

At Preston Gates, the hunt for new Republican talent was also a priority: Abramoff, who had been touted by Jonathan Blank, the firm's managing partner, seemed to fit the bill despite his lack of Capitol Hill experience. Blank and Abramoff had for several years lived across the street from each other on Wood-side Parkway, a quiet, tree-lined residential street in suburban Silver Spring, Maryland, about thirty minutes from downtown D.C. The two men had also become better acquainted through the local Woodside Synagogue, which they both attended. But before the firm hired Abramoff, it undertook a thorough check of his conservative and GOP credentials. After contacting several key offices on Capitol Hill, the lawyers were impressed. "We did due diligence and we were convinced that Jack was highly credible with the GOP people who had come to power," recalled one former colleague.

To be sure, Abramoff's credibility with the new GOP leaders and the conservative movement had much to do with his long-standing political friendship with Norquist from the time they worked together in the early 1980s at College Republicans. A key architect of the Contract with America and a close confi-dant of House Speaker Newt Gingrich, Norquist championed Abramoff's clients and Abramoff's fund-raising for the GOP, which proved invaluable to the neophyte lobbyist. Norquist, who launched Americans for Tax Reform in the mid-1980s, saw his star rise in the wake of the 1994 elections. During the 1994 campaigns, Norquist was instrumental in building grassroots conservative backing and turnout for many GOP candidates who scored victories in the November elections. Norquist has attrib-uted much of the GOP's success in 1994 to what he likes to call the "leave us alone" coalition—a loose but powerful amalgam of conservatives that has included evangelical Christians, pro-gun activists, and antitax crusaders. In a similar vein, Norquist has famously said that for over a quarter century or so he aspired to shrink government in half through tax cuts, less regulation, and other means so that "we can drown it in the bathtub."

To boost Abramoff's lobbying career after the elections, Norquist wrote letters to DeLay and Gingrich heralding Abramoff's arrival as a lobbyist and his yeomanly efforts to expand the GOP presence on K Street and donations to Republicans. In a brief note to DeLay in late February 1995, Norquist suggested to the new majority whip that it "would probably be worthwhile for Jack Abramoff to stop by and brief you on the 'K' Street project," according to a copy of the missive. Abramoff, he added, is "moving his clients to help our side, both through PACs and through giving to our coalition groups."

"Grover gave Abramoff priceless credentials as a conservative lobbyist loyal to conservative Republican causes," in the eyes of J. Michael Waller, a onetime participant in the Americans for Tax Reform weekly meetings and a vice president of the conservative Center for Security Policy. Every Wednesday morning, dozens of Washington's best-known conservative activists from think tanks such as the Heritage Foundation and lobbying powerhouses such as the National Rifle Association (which incidentally boasts Norquist as a board member) have long assembled for a couple of hours of talk about GOP priorities and conservative issues at the offices of ATR.

The meetings, which historically have drawn well-known conservative members from the House and the Senate, top leadership aides, and, in more recent years, such Bush administration stars as Karl Rove, have proved important for networking purposes and keeping in touch with legislative and lobbying priorities. Marshall Wittmann recalled that in the mid-1990s Norquist's weekly strategy sessions devoted inordinate attention to the Marianas as an issue that conservatives ought to embrace. "The Marianas became a great cause célèbre shortly after the Republicans took power," he told me.

Some other conservatives who attended these get-togethers in the mid-1990s were surprised and dismayed at how much attention Abramoff's clients had started to receive. "This was allegedly a meeting about conservative principles," said a conservative think tank official who drifted away from the ATR meetings. "Instead it turned into a freak show. You had the gaming tribes and the sweatshop masters. It was absurd. That's why I stopped going." Michael Waller told me that in some cases, "ATR was acting as a front organization for some of Abramoff's clients and operations."

But other old associates of Abramoff's lobbying career see synergies between his major clients and the conservative movement where his roots were and don't seem surprised that his clients were embraced by many conservatives. "The thing that distinguished Abramoff's lobbying career was that, to a remarkable degree, he was able to choose clients that were consistent with his own ideology," observed Paul Erickson, Abramoff's old friend from College Republican days.

Jack Abramoff's conservative ideology was shaped early during his college days, but in some respects it went back to his childhood and upbringing, first in suburban New Jersey and then Beverly Hills, California. Born in Atlantic City in 1958, Abramoff spent his early childhood in Margate, New Jersey, not far from the famous East Coast gambling center and the Jersey Shore. Abramoff's father, Frank, was a longtime and successful executive with the credit card company Diners Club, who moved the family west to Beverly Hills when Abramoff was still in elementary school. Early on, Abramoff was influenced by one of his father's other jobs, running a business owned by legendary golf champion Arnold Palmer. Former colleagues of the lobbyist say that he liked to regale them with stories about his dad and Palmer. The lobbyist even told some of his associates that his early political views were shaped in part by his family's contacts with Palmer, who was well known for his conservative political stands.

At the age of twelve, Abramoff became involved with Orthodox Judaism, not long after he went to see the movie *Fiddler on the Roof*. By his own account, the film inspired him to study his Jewish religious heritage: he started to learn Hebrew, went·to temple every Saturday, and became a serious follower of Jewish rituals and holidays. A sports buff, Abramoff attended Beverly Hills High School, where he was a star athlete, playing center on his football team and lifting weights.

For college, Abramoff moved back east and, in keeping with his interest in Judaism, attended Brandeis, where he majored in English and became intensely involved for the first time in conservative politics. It was at Brandeis during Reagan's 1980 presidential campaign that Abramoff first met Norquist, a recent graduate of Harvard College who was getting an MBA at Harvard Business School. Abramoff and Norquist struck up a political and personal friendship as they worked closely together to drum up support and student votes for their conservative hero in the liberal Boston environs, efforts that ultimately helped Reagan score an upset win in the state.

Not everything went smoothly for the young conservative organizers. At one event in the suburb of Brookline, Norquist and Abramoff were asked to give some tips to Maureen Reagan, the daughter of the former California governor and presidential candidate, who was coming to town to meet with a group of influential rabbis whose political help the campaign was seeking.

Reagan's daughter was a last-minute substitute and received some quick coaching by Abramoff and Norquist about how to work the crowd of Orthodox Jewish leaders—and about what not to do. But she apparently didn't follow their script: Maureen Reagan attempted to shake hands with the rabbis, a practice verboten to all females (except for spouses), which left the Jewish gathering perplexed and frazzled.

Still, former colleagues of Abramoff and Norquist recall that overall the two men bonded successfully through politics as they worked together to organize several student events and rallies.

Abramoff and Norquist would later take credit for registering and turning out sixteen thousand student votes for Reagan in the state—several times his 3,800-vote margin of victory.

The following year, with Reagan now ensconced in the White House, both Abramoff and Norquist moved to Washington and quickly teamed up to reshape and radicalize College Republicans. An influential training ground for future GOP leaders whose earlier leaders included Karl Rove and Lee Atwater, the group had long had a moderate and somewhat sleepy reputation. Norquist ran Abramoff's successful $10,000 campaign to become chairman of the College Republicans and then worked under him for a couple of years as they transformed the organization by opening new chapters and incorporating a more aggressive, in-your-face style into its programs. The College Republicans enjoyed explosive growth during the four years that Abramoff was chairman. The number of local chapters soared from some two hundred to more than a thousand.

Under Abramoff's stewardship, the College Republicans became known for their increasingly confrontational tactics, which caused some of their more moderate elders to worry about the group's direction. "Our job is to remove liberals" from power, Abramoff wrote at the time, referring to such academic areas as student-run newspapers, radio stations, and governments. "We are replacing those leftists with committed conservatives." Abramoff also distributed to colleges some nine hundred copies of *Target America*, a book that propounded the theory that the Soviet Union had infiltrated the American media with four thousand journalist-agents who were pushing a "massive secret propaganda campaign."

Ralph Reed, a recent graduate of the University of Georgia, came on board in 1983 as the group's executive director. He developed close ties with Abramoff and worked hard to push the group into its intensely combative political mode. Reed helped pen a training brochure for the group that referred to consumer advocate Ralph Nader's network of campus-based public-interest research groups as "tyrannical" and "radical." As they became close friends in Washington, fighting on the front lines for a resurgent conservative movement, Reed famously slept on Abramoff's couch when he first arrived in the capital; a few years later, Reed introduced Abramoff to a fellow Georgian, Pam Alexander, who was to become Abramoff's wife.

During his four years at College Republicans, Abramoff earned a reputation as someone with few qualms about taking risks or playing fast and loose with the rules. Rich Bond, a former chairman of the Republican National Committee, which at the time oversaw the operations of College Republicans, has some unpleasant memories of how Abramoff flouted procedures and ran up a huge debt to boot. Bond recalled that Abramoff conducted an "unauthorized" direct mail campaign by hiring vendors for printing and mailing without going through the normal channels. "The mailing was a colossal flop," Bond told me, adding that it busted their budget and left the RNC with a big bill of just over $100,000 to pay. In retaliation, Bond said, he called Abramoff into his office, looked him in the eye, and proceeded to tell the youthful activist that he had "betrayed [your] standing with the organization. I told him you can't be trusted. It was a good indicator of what a scuz he was."

Other veterans of the RNC have similar early memories of problems with Abramoff's zealousness and disregard for norms. "They never paid their bills on time," recalled Bill Greener, a former director of communications at the RNC. "And they cut corners . . . You lose the moral high ground when you start rationalizing away things that you shouldn't be doing."

After finishing a four-year stint at College Republicans, Abramoff moved on to serve as executive director of another conservative redoubt, Citizens for America, a pro-Reagan civic organization that, among other things, tried to build backing for the Nicaraguan contras. Joining Abramoff at CFA was Norquist, who served as the group's field director. The two men teamed up to persuade the group's founder and chairman, drugstore mogul Lewis Lehrman, to convene an international conference in Africa of anticommunist "freedom fighters" from such far-flung hot spots as Nicaragua, Laos, Mozambique, and Angola.

Abramoff, Norquist, and dozens of other Reagan-era champions of these groups, some of whom had unsavory reputations for human rights abuses, flew into the Angolan city of Jamba for the unusual conservative summit, which was hosted by Jonas Savimbi, the Angolan rebel leader who boasted close ties to the Reagan administration. Notwithstanding the media attention the event garnered, the summit was quickly followed by embarrassing financial problems that echoed Abramoff's experience at College Republicans. Shortly after the conference concluded, Abramoff, Norquist, and five other staffers had a falling-out with Lehrman over financial transactions that reportedly left the group $3 million in the hole. Lehrman had them all sacked.

In the midst of his globe-trotting and the turmoil with Lehrman's group, Abramoff, who had been enrolled in law school at night in Georgetown University Law Center, picked up a degree. But Abramoff never became a member of the D.C. bar.

The next year, Abramoff became executive director of another Washington-based conservative think tank, the International Freedom Foundation. The group, which Abramoff ran for about a year, touted its mission broadly as anticommunism. But the "foundation" focused heavily on undermining the credentials of several major opponents of South Africa's apartheid regime, including Nelson Mandela, who was in jail at the time, and Oliver Tambo, two key leaders of the African National Congress, whom it tried to paint as terrorists and communist sympathizers. It was later revealed that the foundation was part of a political

warfare drive by intelligence operatives in the South African government who covertly funded the effort to the tune of $1.5 mil-
lion annually through 1992, according to sworn testimony to the
South African Truth and Reconciliation Commission. Code-
named "Operation Babushka," the foundation tried to build
backing and burnish the image of the apartheid government in
part by getting Washington conservatives such as Republican
House members Dan Burton of Indiana and Bob Dornan of California to attend some of its forums.

Not long afterward, Abramoff's career took a detour of sorts
through Hollywood, where he worked on a film project that embodied the young conservative warrior's political perspective.
Over the next few years, Abramoff teamed up with his brother
Robert, his old friend Paul Erickson, and a few other colleagues
to make *Red Scorpion*, an anticommunist potboiler loosely pat-
terned after the experiences of Savimbi.

Filmed in Namibia, which was then controlled by South
Africa, and parts of Angola, *Red Scorpion* was coauthored and
produced by Abramoff and starred Swedish actor Dolph Lundgren. It was plainly a labor of love for the young conservatives,
who had scant experience in moviemaking. Erickson recalled
that he and Abramoff started out by reading a primer on film-
making. Erickson said that the Angola filming benefited from
some logistical help provided by Savimbi's rebels, and he recalled at least one occasion that the filming was interrupted because of attacks nearby by Marxist opponents. By the time the
film was released in 1989 it had cost close to $17 million, ac-
cording to Erickson. *Newsday* has quoted a former South African
intelligence officer familiar with Abramoff's ties to the apartheid
government as saying that *Red Scorpion* was "funded by our
guys." Abramoff has vigorously denied this and said that funding
came from private investors.

For all their hard work, the critics weren't kind to the movie.

It's not hard to see why, based on the plot and some of the dialogue. Lundgren played Nikolai, a burly and brutal Russian commando with a fondness for killing, vodka, and belching. In one infamous scene, Lundgren swipes a machine gun from a policeman in a bar and proceeds to shoot up the whole bar. A reviewer for *The Washington Post* panned the movie as "basically a comic book or a Saturday morning cartoon masquerading as a feature film."

Abramoff's time in South Africa, though, did yield some long-term political friendships. It was during the filming of *Red Scorpion* that Abramoff struck up a friendship with two well-known conservative South African rabbis: David and Daniel Lapin. The two brothers moved to the United States in the 1990s, and during Abramoff's lobbying career, both played intriguing small behind-the-scenes roles.

In the early 1990s, a few years before Abramoff got into the lobbying business, he briefly played a cameo part trying to help his father, Frank, land a foreign casino deal in the Marianas. The elder Abramoff was seeking a license for a gambling venture he wanted to open in Tinian, one of the Marianas, but ran into stiff opposition from a gaming board in the islands that had to approve it. Fred Gushin, who served formerly as an adviser to the gaming commission on Tinian, remembers that Frank Abramoff's application was never acted on but adds that if the commission had made a formal ruling he believes it would have nixed the application because of "significant evidence that Abramoff's father lacked adequate financing." Eventually, with prospects for the application fading, Gushin said that he received two or three calls from Jack Abramoff, who tried to lobby him on behalf of his father's project in the Marianas. The son's efforts were rebuffed, Gushin informed me.

Nevertheless, the senior Abramoff proved influential a few years later as his son was starting to hunt for his first clients in

Washington. According to former colleagues, in early 1995, Abramoff's father had a hand in making an introduction that helped his son sign up his first client, the Mississippi Choctaws. "Jack's father had a Rolodex and he knew how to use it," recalled one of Abramoff's former colleagues. "His father was making calls for Jack to help him get going."

From the start of his career, Abramoff focused intently on landing lobbying clients with the resources to pay him very large fees and make him a star rainmaker who could rival the city's biggest revenue producers. Abramoff was more interested in representing a handful of well-heeled clients than in building a broad practice, according to former lobbying associates, and he generally eschewed work for major companies with Washington offices that might look over his shoulder. "He wanted clients where there was a lot at stake, so they could support a large financial effort," recalls a lobbyist who worked with him at Preston Gates. "Jack wanted to be number one in the city. He wanted to top Tommy Boggs," the city's most powerful Democratic lobbyist, who for almost three decades had been a name partner with the very successful firm of Patton Boggs.

Abramoff's hard-driving and high-profile style sometimes clashed with the more conservative style of Preston Gates veterans, who preferred to keep lower profiles and regarded their new star colleague as too brash and ruthless. "Jack was very affected by athletics," recalled one of his ex–lobbying associates. "Winning was everything for Jack." And Abramoff, the high school athlete, liked to use sports metaphors to rally his lobbying associates to greater action, stressing that "everybody on the team had a role to play."

But there was no doubt that the team was captained by Abramoff, who worked tirelessly to forge strong ties with key House members and their top aides. Those efforts kept Abramoff busy wining and dining new recruits, who sometimes got treated to golf outings in the Washington area or taken on trips to meet his clients, such as the Choctaws or the Marianas.

The core of the lobbying team that Abramoff built included several former House leadership aides with GOP pedigrees and a couple of Democrats. Abramoff early on recruited Bill Jarrell, who joined the firm in 1997 after a few years in DeLay's office where he was deputy chief of staff; Dennis Stephens, a onetime top aide to two other Texans, representatives Dick Armey and Joe Barton; and Pat Pizzella, a former official at the Education Department.

Later on, "team Abramoff," as it was called inside the firm, would expand with other young conservative stalwarts such as Kevin Ring, who had been with John Doolittle of California, a close DeLay ally, and Shawn Vasell, who had spent a few years with Conrad Burns of Montana. Most of the Hill aides recruited by Abramoff were in their late twenties or early thirties and seemed drawn to the lobbying world by his flamboyant, hard-driving style and lavish spending.

"Jack looked for staffers to up-and-coming members," recalled one ex–leadership aide who was familiar with Abramoff's modus operandi. "He wanted staffers who were aggressive and highly social, who were impressed by important people." But some of these fledgling lobbyists soon developed an "entitlement mind-set. They wanted their piece and forgot why they had come to Washington."

Abramoff's first years at Preston Gates were in several respects a harbinger of his career to come. His biggest clients, the Choctaws and the Marianas, were financial angels that Abramoff tapped for hundreds of thousands of dollars for political projects for DeLay and his conservative allies. Early on, Abramoff's team not only scored victories for the Choctaws by blocking two congressional efforts in 1995 and again in 1997 to tax Indian casino revenues but also helped fend off potential gambling competition in Alabama and secured congressional appropriations for a few tribal priorities.

One such victory that Abramoff notched for the Choctaws occurred in 1997 when he lobbied hard to get Senator Thad Cochran, a Mississippi Republican, to insert a sentence of nineteen words into a mammoth appropriations bill that exempted the tribe from regulatory scrutiny by the National Indian Gaming Commission. Cochran's legislative maneuver also allowed the Mississippi tribe to avoid the fees that the gaming body levied on other tribes, which saved the Choctaws about $180,000 a year.

From the mid-1990s through 2002, almost $1.5 million from the Choctaws went to ATR. Of that total, Norquist's ATR banked close to $350,000 from the Choctaws; $1.15 million was funneled by ATR to Ralph Reed to lead a drive that began in 1999 against an Alabama lottery referendum on the ballot that year and a video poker measure pending in the legislature in 2000; if either the statewide lottery or the poker measure had been approved, it would have posed economic threats to the Choctaws, whose casino in Philadelphia, Mississippi, drew lots of business from Alabamans.

In his successful drive to blunt new gaming in Alabama, Abramoff early on realized that it would be useful to have organized support from the state's social and religious conservatives, a job that Reed was well suited to spearhead. A former colleague of Abramoff's told me that the lobbyist "viewed alliances between casino owners and ministers" as powerful lobbying tools. But to protect Reed's image as an antigambling conservative, Abramoff needed to hide the source of the funds—and that's where Norquist's organization came in handy and made some money to boot. Abramoff persuaded Norquist to let him use ATR as a conduit for funneling funds to two Alabama groups that paid Reed's Atlanta-based consulting company, Century

Strategies, to spearhead the antigambling drive. Over a two-year period, the Choctaws sent $1.15 million through ATR to the Alabama Christian Coalition and Citizens Against Legalized Lottery of Birmingham to help run the successful antigambling drive. Reed kept the Alabama Christian Coalition, which received $850,000 of the funds, in the dark about the funds coming from the Mississippi tribe, a potential embarrassment for the antigambling group. The Choctaws later issued a statement that the funds they used came from their nongambling revenues.

According to documents released by Senate investigators, Reed was kept apprised of how Abramoff was using Norquist's group as a conduit to protect him from disclosure. In one Abramoff e-mail message on February 7, 2000, the lobbyist cautioned Reed that he might not get quite as much as he anticipated for his campaign because "I need to give Grover something for [helping], so the first transfer will be a bit lighter." Later that month, Abramoff sent himself an e-mail expressing surprise that "Grover kept another 25K." Not long after the e-mails were disclosed by the Indian Affairs Committee, Norquist defended his actions to *Time* magazine by noting that the Choctaws had twice authorized him to take $25,000. But Norquist in some of his e-mails to Abramoff showed his eagerness for Choctaw cash. In a May 1999 e-mail, Norquist asked him: "What is the status of the Choctaw stuff? I have a $75g hole in my budget from last year. Ouch."

While the Choctaw-financed work was helpful to Reed as he was launching his career as a corporate consultant, it remained politically sensitive. During his tenure at the Christian Coalition, Reed had long trumpeted his antigambling stance, referring to gambling as a "cancer on the American body politic." And despite Reed's repeated efforts to distance himself from Abramoff's tribal clients, e-mails released by the Senate Indian Affairs Committee indicate clearly that Abramoff had informed

Reed at the time that he was getting funding from the Choctaws.

In one such e-mail, Abramoff pointedly told Reed that he was contacting an official of the Choctaws named Nell Rogers to make sure that Reed was paid promptly for his work for the tribe. In an e-mail dated March 29, 1999, Abramoff informed Reed with regard to a request of his for hundreds of thousands of dollars that "they are not scared by the number . . . But want to know precisely what you are planning to do." A few days later, on April 4, in another e-mail to Reed, Abramoff informed the Georgian that once he received Reed's itemized expenses, he would "call Nell at Choctaw and get it approved." In yet another Abramoff e-mail to Reed in 1999, the lobbyist urged him "to get me invoices as soon as possible so I can get Choctaw to get us checks asap."

Norquist's group provided other help to the Choctaws and seemed to benefit financially in other ways from Abramoff's Indian casino work. According to former colleagues of Abramoff, Norquist took at least one trip down to see the casino and arranged for ATR to give an award one year to Chief Phillip Martin of the Choctaws. More important, Norquist's group produced a study written by Peter Ferrara, a conservative economist and consultant to ATR, which touted the benefits of gambling for tribal economics and was widely disseminated in conservative circles.

In turn, Abramoff invited Norquist to Preston Gates in early 1997 to make a pitch for financial help for his group to Martin and a representative of the Chitimacha, a Louisiana tribe that Abramoff was trying to sign up as a client. To prep Norquist for the meeting, Abramoff put together some talking points. "The message is that the Choctaws can't do this alone," Abramoff suggested in his missive. He also reminded Norquist to praise the Choctaws and noted they "were kind enough to provide resources" to ATR in the 1995 fight when the two old friends worked together to kill a bill in conference that would have taxed the Choctaws' casino revenues. And, in a fitting coda, Abramoff advised Norquist that "it would be a big help if you could laud Chief Martin [of the Choctaws] for all he has done."

As Abramoff was fast establishing his credentials on K Street, the Choctaws were one of a few clients along with the Marianas that helped him build his reputation for lavish entertaining, travel, and fund-raising power. And no office on Capitol Hill benefited as handsomely as did DeLay's. Both the Choctaws' casino and golf resort and the Marianas combined vacation and lobbying opportunities that Abramoff used in part to wine and dine members and Hill staffers, including some of DeLay's top staff such as Ed Buckham, his chief of staff, and Tony Rudy, his deputy chief of staff. In the late 1990s, Abramoff's firm organized about two dozen trips to the Marianas for members, staffers, and conservative activists, where good beaches and well-manicured golf courses offered Washington power brokers enticing getaways and gave Abramoff or his associates a chance to sell the Marianas and its garment industry as economic success stories.

In 1997 and early 1998, Abramoff helped to arrange two junkets to the Marianas and to Moscow for DeLay, Ed Buckham, and other top staffers to meet key clients in very convivial settings with lots of golf and good food. "Foreign trips were part of the work-hard, play-hard DeLay philosophy," recalled a former Abramoff associate. "To that end, Abramoff was director of travel for DeLay Inc."

The Moscow trip, which took place in August of 1997, was sponsored officially by a conservative think tank called the National Center for Public Policy Research that was run by an old friend of Abramoff's, Amy Ridenour, whom he'd known from College Republicans. The six-day trip, which cost just over $57,000, featured meetings with then prime minister Viktor

Chernomyrdin and Russian religious leaders, and some golf on the side. According to DeLay's official travel reports filed with Congress, the center was sponsor of the Moscow trip, but sources told me that the costs were actually picked up by a Bahamas-based client of Abramoff's, Chelsea Commercial Enterprises, which had ties to the Russian energy firm Naftasib.

Abramoff's mission for Chelsea Commercial, according to lobbying reports he filed, was a broad one: to promote policies favorable to the Russian government, including "progressive market reforms and trade with the United States." During their stay in Moscow, DeLay, Buckham, and Abramoff were guests at an opulent dinner party thrown for them by two top executives with Naftasib, Alexander Koulakovsky and Marina Nevskaya. Koulakovsky, the firm's general manager, escorted DeLay around Moscow during part of his visit. DeLay's office has defended the trip and said that its main purpose was to meet with Russian religious leaders.

Naftasib was a midsize Russian energy and construction firm that was politically well connected in Russia, boasting contracts with the Ministry of Defense and financial investments in Russian energy giant Gazprom. With criminal violence becoming endemic for many Russian businesses, part of Naftasib's agenda was to raise its profile with prominent Washington politicians like DeLay in an effort to lessen the risks of any personal attacks on its top executives, including Koulakovsky and Nevskaya. In addition, the firm's agenda in Washington included obtaining financial and other backing to help Naftasib build middle-class modular housing projects in Moscow and garnering support for a proposed fossil fuel project in Israel. Neither of these projects was ever accomplished.

During the Marianas trip, which occurred over New Year's at the start of 1998, DeLay promised the islands that he would block any efforts to end their much-prized exemption from U.S.

minimum wage rules and other workplace regulations. It was on this trip too that DeLay attended a fancy dinner party hosted by textile industry tycoon Willie Tan and very publicly referred to Abramoff as "one of my closest and dearest friends" and "your most able representative in Washington." DeLay further advised his wealthy hosts to "stand firm" for their cause and summed up his support for the Marianas with the message: "Resist evil. Remember that all truth and blessings emanate from our creator."

DeLay was instrumental in blocking several efforts to impose U.S. labor and minimum wage laws on the islands' garment manufacturers, whose exports to the United States came to about $1 billion a year. DeLay famously lauded the islands as a "perfect petri dish of capitalism," and my "own Galapagos Islands" in an interview in 2000 with *The Washington Post*.

That view was certainly shared and reinforced by Abramoff's Marianas lobbying. In one particularly striking rhetorical leap, Abramoff even compared Democratic proposals to impose U.S. labor laws on the Marianas to the Nuremberg Laws, which were one of the most odious symbols of Nazi Germany's oppression of Jews. "These are immoral laws designed to destroy the economic lives of a people," Abramoff warned conservatives about Democratic proposals. He added that conservatives see in this "battle a microcosm of an overall battle . . . What these guys in the CNMI are trying to build is a life without being wards of the state."

Tan and the Marianas, which had a population of only 53,000, had long faced a tough battle to keep their exemptions from minimum wage laws and other labor rules. In 1991, five garment companies owned by Tan were hit with a lawsuit by the U.S. Labor Department that charged them with sweatshop conditions, including employees being forced to work eighty-four hours a week without overtime and sometimes being locked in their worksites. Tan wound up paying $9 million to twelve hundred workers to settle the suit, the largest ever filed by the Labor Department.

Besides helping to underwrite these lavish trips, at Abramoff's behest these same clients became sugar daddies for DeLay's political operation, in which Buckham was the central figure. Buckham, a lay minister and a well-connected Washington evangelical figure, was both DeLay's chief of staff and a spiritual adviser. From the start of his lobbying, Abramoff focused much of his energies on building personal ties to DeLay's staff through shared passions for everything from golf to racquetball to sushi. Abramoff's wooing of the DeLay staff started with Buckham and later included other top staffers like Tony Rudy, who became deputy chief of staff, and Michael Scanlon, his communications director.

Probably no project was more important to Abramoff's long-term goal of boosting the fortunes of DeLay—and his own standing with the Texan and Buckham—than the U.S. Family Network, a low-profile nonprofit advocacy group that was set up in 1996 by Buckham while he was still DeLay's chief of staff. "Buckham was the gatekeeper to DeLay," said a former high-level leadership aide who knew the office and Abramoff well. "Ed was the puppet master in terms of the evangelical side and contact with that community. He was constantly harping on the need to pump up the base."

To ingratiate himself with DeLay, Abramoff banked heavily on Buckham, who was extremely close personally and politically to the Texan. A born-again evangelical from Tennessee, Buckham had a smooth-as-molasses speaking style and an easy laugh. In some ways, Buckham's religious fervor mirrored Abramoff's Orthodox Judaism and created a bond between the two men similar to the ties between the lobbyist and Ralph Reed.

From 1996 to 2001, the network received the lion's share of its $3.0 million in funding from three large Abramoff clients or allied financial interests, all of which DeLay had backed in different ways. At the peak of the network's fund-raising success in 1998, the Mississippi Choctaws; Willie Tan, the Marianas garment executive who was very close to the island's government; and a London law firm that reportedly had links to the Russian oil and gas industry executives and their company Naftasib poured $1.8 million into the group's coffers. The largest single contribution to the network in 1998 came from the London law firm of James & Sarch, which chipped in $1 million. In 2000, James & Sarch went out of business.

During its five years of operation, the network was overseen by a small board that was composed of several evangelical ministers. One of these was pastor Christopher Geeslin of Frederick, Maryland, who was both a personal friend and minister to Buckham. Geeslin, who served from 1998 to 2001 as a director or president of the network, later became deeply disillusioned with Buckham after he learned more about the sources of the group's funding by Abramoff clients and related interests.

A bearded, soft-spoken man in his early fifties, Geeslin told me that in 1998 Buckham boasted to him that the $1 million contribution to the network, which purportedly came from James & Sarch in London, actually was made by Russian "energy barons," whom he later understood were connected to Naftasib. Geeslin recalled Buckham telling him that the donation from the Russians was given to influence a DeLay vote on legislation then pending in Congress to replenish IMF funding, which would help the troubled Russian economy and wealthy Russians.

A spokesman for DeLay, who voted for the IMF legislation even though many of his GOP colleagues criticized it, has said that his vote was based on the merits of the issue and had nothing to do with any donations. Nevskaya has told *The Washington Post*, which has also cited Geeslin and another unnamed source familiar with Buckham as saying that Russian energy interests were behind the $1 million donation, that neither Naftasib, she, nor Koulakovsky had anything to do with the contribution.

The network touted itself as a grassroots organization aimed at promoting "moral fitness" and a pro-family agenda; DeLay personally signed a fund-raising letter for the group in 1999, calling it "a powerful nationwide organization dedicated to restoring our government to citizen control." But the group actually spent only a small fraction of the $3.0 million it raised on real grassroots advocacy programs. Almost a third of its funds went to Buckham and the Alexander Strategy Group, a fledgling lobbying firm that he launched in late 1997 when he was leaving DeLay's office. These funds were certainly very helpful in getting Alexander Strategy Group off the ground: Buckham's firm had only one lobbying client, the Hebrew Vocational Institute, during his first full year of operations in 1998.

The network bought a $429,000 Capitol Hill town house that housed its one-person office. The town house also provided space for almost two years to both Alexander Strategy and DeLay's PAC, Americans for a Republican Majority, which Buckham also helped run after he left the congressman's office. DeLay himself used the town house, which was referred to as his "safe house," to make fund-raising calls for ARMPAC. The network, according to its tax records and Geeslin, also invested in some pricey art for decorative purposes: it spent almost $62,375 in 1999 on Salvador Dalí and Peter Max artwork, some of which adorned the town house's walls.

The network had a formal financial arrangement with Buckham and Alexander Strategy that was first codified in late 1997 in an agreement that Buckham signed when he was still working for DeLay. Under the agreement, Alexander Strategy Group was to receive a monthly retainer of $12,000 plus fees of up to 15 percent of all large donations that the network received. The payments to the firm started in October 1997, just before Buckham actually left DeLay's office in December.

Starting in 1998 too, Christine DeLay, the wife of the congressman, received a monthly consulting fee that ranged from

$3,200 to $3,400 to do research on the favorite charities of members of Congress and consult for ARMPAC. That arrangement lasted for three years and paid her a total of $115,000. Buckham's wife, Wendy, who served briefly on the board of the Family Network and did its books for a few years, also received consulting fees that totaled $43,000 during 1997 when, her husband was still DeLay's chief of staff. Three times that year, as part of her overall compensation, Wendy Buckham received a check for $10,000, each coming on the same day, or soon after, the network banked a large contribution from one of Abramoff's clients or allies.

It was certainly no coincidence that some of the network's bigger donations from Abramoff's clients also came on the heels of meetings with DeLay or his wife and top staff. On July 18, 1997, for instance, just a few weeks before DeLay's trip to Moscow, Koulakovsky attended a luncheon in Houston that drew about ten local oil and gas executives as well as Abramoff, Christine DeLay, and Susan Hirschmann, DeLay's deputy chief of staff. It's unclear whether the meeting led to any business deals between the Russians and their American counterparts, or was just intended to flaunt Abramoff's connections to impress the Russian. On July 24, the network received its largest donation in 1997, a check for $250,000 from James & Sarch, which reportedly was used to funnel funds from the Russian energy executives to the family network.

Richard Cullen, an attorney for DeLay, told me that he didn't know who arranged the meeting. Cullen explained that at the last minute the congressman had obligations that kept him in Washington, and DeLay asked his wife to attend in his place. DeLay, Cullen added, "viewed the [meeting] as a routine way to showcase Houston to business leaders interested in expanding trade."

This wasn't the only time that a large check to the network closely followed a meeting involving DeLay or his top staffers with an Abramoff client. In the summer of 1998, DeLay, his wife, and Susan Hirschmann spent a few days visiting the Choctaws on a trip that according to their House travel records was aimed at assessing a Choctaw site that the congressman was considering as a place to hold a charity golf event to benefit his foundation. The golf event was never held there, but according to the network's tax records, just a day after the DeLays left, a check for $150,000 from the Choctaws arrived for the family group's coffers.

In February of 2006, J. Thomas Smith, a former counsel for the U.S. Family Network, received an FBI subpoena requesting a variety of records and documents relating to any dealings that the group had with Koulakovsky, Nevskaya, Naftasib, the Choctaws, and Tan Holdings. The subpoena also asked for documents and records concerning Ed and Wendy Buckham, Tom and Christine DeLay, and Jack Abramoff, among others.

To a large extent, the network seemed to be a conduit for Abramoff clients that had strong ties to DeLay to underwrite projects that would benefit the Texan—and Buckham, as he moved from DeLay's office into lobbying. "Jack reassured Buckham that he could help him" as he was moving into the lobbying world, recalled a former lobbying associate of Abramoff's. "When Ed left, he wasted little time in capitalizing on his relationship with Jack," recalled one ex–leadership aide who knew both men. "Jack needed Ed for access to DeLay, and Ed needed Jack for his business acumen."

Looking back on the network's operations, Geeslin recalled in a few interviews that he was "naïve" about the sources of funding that the Family Network was receiving. "We weren't the most vigilant board," he told me with a trace of embarrassment. "We really trusted Ed. He was working for our evangelical star, Tom DeLay." But slowly, Geeslin said, some of the funds, including some $650,000 from garment industry executives in the Marianas, principally Willie Tan, became sources of friction and stirred bitterness. Geeslin grew particularly upset that Buckham had simply dismissed questions that he and others raised about published reports of poor working conditions, forced abortions, and forced prostitution in the Marianas. Subsequently, Geeslin was dismayed to learn that the stories of these abuses in the Marianas were largely true and that, in addition, Abramoff had paid some conservative journalists thousands of dollars to write positive pieces about conditions in the Marianas. Also early on, Geeslin suggested to Buckham that it might be worthwhile to send an evangelical mission to the Marianas to minister to people who worked in the garment industry. But after initially voicing interest in the idea, Buckham apparently had second thoughts and nothing ever came of the proposal. "We were used big-time by Buckham," Geeslin said with some bitterness.

Buckham, though, was apparently willing to go the extra mile, to help Abramoff in the Marianas with sensitive political missions. In early December 1999, Buckham went to the Marianas with Michael Scanlon, who was about to leave DeLay's office to join Abramoff at Preston Gates, on a highly unusual and delicate mission that combined politics with lobbying. The Marianas trip came at a critical moment for Abramoff, whose contract with the island had expired about a year before and which he had been working zealously to get renewed. To achieve his goal, Abramoff was pinning his hopes on Benigno Fitial, a former high-level garment industry executive and political ally who was in a tough race to become speaker of the Marianas House of Delegates, a powerful position in the islands.

Fitial's loyalty to Abramoff and DeLay was well known. In April 1997, Fitial played golf with DeLay at a Houston charity event to benefit the DeLay Foundation for Kids and then came to Washington to lobby Congress on the Marianas' labor issues that Abramoff was pressing. Right after his Washington visit, Fitial sent Buckham an effusive e-mail, mentioning that DeLay must have been "happy after the golf tournament because he beat me by one stroke." Fitial too thanked Buckham and DeLay for "allowing our group to virtually take over [DeLay's] office."

The Marianas trip, which also included Neil Volz, then Ney's chief of staff, was a covert drive: Abramoff was especially concerned to hide the funds that paid for it, which came from Willie Tan, and to do so he turned to Ridenour of the National Center for Public Policy Research, according to e-mails released by McCain's committee. In a December 1999 e-mail, Ridenour seemed perfectly willing to let her group serve as a conduit, writing that "we'll call the bank first thing in the a.m. and confirm that the money has arrived, and then I will get checks out to you and Ed." In an e-mail to Susan Ralston, his chief assistant at Preston Gates, Abramoff stressed secrecy in paying for the "very important" trip. "The tickets should not in any way say my name or our firm's name," Abramoff wrote. "They should, if possible, say National Center for Public Policy Research. We should pay using my Visa." The plea bargains of Abramoff, Scanlon, and Volz all cited the trip as an illegal activity.

To help Fitial win the speaker's job in early 2000, Buckham and Scanlon's task was to persuade two Democrats to switch their votes and back the Abramoff ally: the effort succeeded after Buckham and Scanlon met with the two wavering legislators and told them that if they voted for Fitial, the prospects for new congressional appropriations for infrastructure projects in their districts would be greatly enhanced. The *Los Angeles Times* has reported that both legislators, Alejo Mendiola and Norman Palacios, were promised help with their pet projects if they backed Fitial. Palacios, who wanted help with appropriations to repair a run-down breakwater on the island of Tinian, was gratified when in October 2000 Congress passed an energy and water appropriations bill that contained $150,000 for the initial restoration of the breakwater. DeLay, who served on the House Appropriations

Committee at the time, was part of the conference that approved the Tinian funding.

For his part, Fitial moved quickly after he won the speaker's job in early 2000 to press other officials to renew Abramoff's contract. In late June 2000, Fitial sent an e-mail to a key aide to the island's governor, Pedro Tenorio, which said that "we need P & G [Abramoff's firm] to help save our economy . . . Please help!!" To expand the pressure, the House of Delegates under Speaker Fitial enacted two resolutions requesting that Abramoff's firm be rehired. Shortly after the second one, the Marianas governor approved a new $100,000-a-month contract for Abramoff.

The help provided in the Marianas by Buckham and Scanlon was a clear indication of the enormous leverage that Abramoff had with DeLay's office through Buckham and other staffers. In Geeslin's eyes, Buckham seemed to be mesmerized by Abramoff. Buckham used to speak of Abramoff as though "he was in awe of him," Geeslin told me. "Ed wanted to emulate Jack. Ed was impressed by his money prowess and his balls at asking people for money."

Buckham's smooth journey from DeLay's office to K Street, which depended heavily on Abramoff's help and his clients' largesse, was just one of the lobbyist's endeavors to further cement his ties to the Texan. Almost simultaneously, Abramoff was working to forge links with Scanlon and Rudy, efforts that in 2000 were going to bear more dividends for the lobbyist and his clients. "To the casual observer it was a pretty simple deal," recalled one former House leadership aide familiar with Abramoff and DeLay. "Jack raised money for the pet projects of DeLay and took care of his top staff. In turn they granted him tremendous access and allowed Abramoff to freely trade on DeLay's name."

THREE

Miami Vice

■

By the turn of the new millennium, most Republicans and Democrats in the Washington lobbying world had heard plenty of buzz about the million-dollar-plus annual fees that Abramoff's firm had been paid for several years by the Choctaws and the Marianas and felt a mix of envy, awe, and puzzlement at just how the lobbyist pulled it off. Abramoff was earning well over $1 million a year from his lobbying practice at Preston Gates, enabling him and his family to move into a much more luxurious home in one of Silver Spring's upscale sections. The lobbyist's house was well furnished with expensive antiques and boasted a pricey golf simulator in the basement. In early July 2000, Abramoff's reputation was further enhanced when *The Wall Street Journal* published a mostly flattering front-page profile of the lobbyist that referred to him as a "GOP stalwart" and included high praise from DeLay for the millions of dollars that Abramoff had corralled for GOP and conservative coffers.

But despite his own financial success and enhanced clout on K Street, Abramoff had been feeling restless and was casting around for bigger challenges that might bring him considerably more money and prestige. "Jack was tired of being merely a middleman" for Indian casinos, a former colleague of Abramoff's told me. "He said we need to be the guys making a million a day."

Right around the start of 2000, serendipitously, one of Abramoff's lobbying associates tipped him off about a profitable fleet of gambling boats in Florida that was up for sale, and he quickly smelled an irresistible opportunity. Art Dimopoulos, a maritime lawyer at Preston Gates, told Abramoff that one of his clients, a Greek immigrant named Konstantinos "Gus" Boulis, was being forced by the government to sell his midsize fleet of gambling ships called SunCruz Casinos, which was raking in $30 million a year.

Boulis, a self-made millionaire who had founded the Miami Subs chain, had been charged by federal prosecutors in 1999 with breaking the U.S. Shipping Act because he had bought the gambling cruise ships without being a U.S. citizen. Under a legal agreement that Boulis struck with prosecutors, he had to pay a $1 million fine. Boulis also had thirty-six months to sell his eleven gambling boats, which were famed for running "cruises to nowhere" a few miles offshore in international waters to avoid a Florida gambling ban. The cruises, which left daily from nine ports in Florida, attracted a wide mix of customers, from tourists and retirees to veteran gamblers and high rollers. Dimopoulos told Abramoff to let him know if he thought of anyone outside the firm who might be interested in buying the lucrative enterprise.

Abramoff apparently thought almost immediately of working on the deal with Adam Kidan, an old friend from College Republicans and a fellow risk taker who liked new business opportunities. Not long before, Kidan and Abramoff had teamed up with another friend from College Republicans, Ben Waldman, to start an unusual and not overly profitable enterprise: a fleet of water taxis on the Potomac that displayed commercial advertising.

For almost a decade, Kidan had been wheeling and dealing in

a motley assortment of businesses with scant success. For several years, Kidan had run a Washington-based Dial-a-Mattress franchise, which had gone into bankruptcy, and in the early 1990s he had owned a bagel business on Long Island that was based in the posh Hamptons. Kidan, a New York native with a law degree from Brooklyn College who also reportedly had ties to a well-known New York mobster, soon told Abramoff that he was game for trying to acquire SunCruz, notwithstanding his lack of financial assets. Ultimately, Waldman, a former Reagan administration official, would also join them in pursuing the acquisition.

Abramoff, according to former associates, was eager to make more money—one remembered that he once talked of his desire to make $1 billion—and SunCruz looked like a golden opportunity. "Jack was totally focused and consumed with owning a gaming company," said one former associate. "He talked about it a lot." SunCruz promised to be "his ticket to riches and his exit from hourly fees," recalled another former associate.

For much of the year, Abramoff spent long hours plotting SunCruz strategy and financing options with Kidan and others, while also working on a few lobbying issues, including an expensive and tough fight for the Internet gaming company eLottery, which wanted to kill a bill that would have banned gambling on the Internet.

But Abramoff's consuming passion for buying SunCruz seemed to dominate much of the year and led to major frictions with his colleagues. Those rifts grew out of Abramoff's decision to embark on the acquisition without informing his Preston Gates colleagues for several months that he intended to be associated with Kidan. The firm faced a conflict because "it could not represent a client in any matter in which an employee had a significant financial stake," recalled a former colleague of Abramoff's.

These tensions were heightened too by the arrival in early 2000 of Abramoff's latest recruit at the firm—Michael Scanlon. Known for being brash and a loose cannon on Capitol Hill, Scanlon joined Preston Gates after much arm twisting by Abramoff himself, who had to overcome strong reservations of some of the firm's senior lobbyists and lawyers and fellow Republicans. Scanlon was generally regarded as a spinmeister and a lightweight. Scanlon had a reputation for creating political headaches on the Hill. "Nobody wanted Mike," recalled one of his former Preston Gates colleagues. "The other Republicans hated him."

It's not hard to see why there was so much anxiety about Scanlon, a preppy-looking and fast-talking man in his late twenties who, after he left DeLay's office, spent some summers at Rehoboth Beach, Delaware, where he worked as a lifeguard. After he departed from Capitol Hill and joined Preston Gates in April 2000, Scanlon was still paying off loans from college. At best, Scanlon had a checkered reputation from his Capitol Hill days, where he had bounced around for a couple of years working in different offices as a press aide before he landed in De-Lay's office in 1997.

On the Hill, Scanlon had also raised eyebrows, even among some conservatives, for his zealousness during the impeachment of Bill Clinton. Former Hill aides recount that Scanlon and Tony Rudy, DeLay's hard-charging deputy chief of staff, were a one-two team working aggressively in what one described as a "renegade blitz" to impeach the president, which caused several rank-and-file members heartburn. Rudy was "running a full whipping operation from his desk," one former leadership aide told me. "Scanlon was taking everything that Tony fed him about Clinton and which members were undecided [about which way to vote] and peddling it to the press." He added that Rudy and Scanlon's actions weren't "sanctioned by leadership, and DeLay looked the other way."

Scanlon's renegade and pugnacious style was well captured in one of his own e-mails that he sent to Rudy, which was cited by *Washington Post* reporter Peter Baker in *The Breach*, his book about the impeachment fight. "This whole thing about not kicking someone when they are down is total B.S. . . . Not only do you kick him—you kick him until he passes out—then beat him over the head with a baseball bat—then roll him up in an old rug—and throw him off a cliff into the pound surf below!!!!"

Not long after his arrival at Preston Gates, Scanlon hurt his image further when, at a firm retreat on the eastern shore of Maryland, he lectured a couple of dozen veteran lobbyists about strategies for pursuing new business opportunities, a subject on which Scanlon was a real neophyte. "It was very embarrassing," recalled a former associate who attended the talk. Equally embarrassing in the eyes of several Abramoff colleagues was the unusual chemistry between the two men. "Mike fed Jack's worst side," remembered a former Preston Gates associate. "Mike could get Jack even more spun up." And another lobbyist told me that the relationship between the two men was often strained. "Jack treated Mike like a thirteen-year-old girlfriend, or a bad habit that he wasn't supposed to have."

But Abramoff didn't have much patience for Scanlon's critics or his own. Even before Scanlon officially started work at Preston Gates, Abramoff had turned to him for help in clinching the SunCruz deal. In the negotiations to buy SunCruz, problems surfaced early for Kidan and Abramoff over the asking price and some terms of the sale. After signing a letter of intent in January 2000 to sell SunCruz for $145 million, Boulis soon was pushing for a side consulting deal and other terms that made the purchase less attractive.

In response, Abramoff and Scanlon started to brainstorm about whom they might approach for political help on Capitol Hill to make the deal more palatable, and they came up with the idea of Bob Ney of Ohio, a close GOP ally of DeLay, with whom they both had good ties. Scanlon was a buddy of Neil Volz, Ney's then chief of staff; they played cards a lot and often hung out after work. Volz agreed to help Scanlon persuade Ney to put a statement in the *Congressional Record* that might cut the sale price by blasting Boulis's track record at SunCruz and his character.

Ney's hard-hitting statement on March 30, 2000, seemed designed to pressure Boulis to cut his price. "Mr. Speaker, how SunCruz Casinos and Gus Boulis conduct themselves with regard to Florida law is very unnerving . . . On the Ohio River we have gaming interests that run clean operations and provide quality entertainment. I don't want to see the actions of one bad apple in Florida, or anywhere else to affect the business aspect of this industry or hurt any innocent casino patron in our country." In June, Ney's campaign committee received $4,000 in contributions from Scanlon, Abramoff, his wife, Pam, and Kidan.

To be sure, Ney wasn't the only well-placed Washington insider whom Abramoff turned to for assistance in buying Sun-Cruz. He asked two other Capitol Hill friends, Tony Rudy and Representative Dana Rohrabacher, to provide personal references with potential lenders, which they both did. Rohrabacher, a California Republican who had known Abramoff since the early 1980s, said he doesn't recall providing a reference, but he told *The Washington Post* in April 2005 that he "would certainly have been happy to give him a good recommendation. He's a very honest man." Rudy, a native of New Jersey and a lawyer who was crazy about ice hockey, provided other vital assistance. In June 2000, Rudy—who in about six months would leave Capitol Hill and become a lobbying associate of Abramoff's—made arrangements to send a flag that had flown over the Capitol to Boulis, a small gesture but one that was no doubt meant to impress the Florida gambling mogul with Abramoff's connections in the capital. Rudy also accompanied

Abramoff, Kidan, and Joan Wagner, the chief financial officer of SunCruz, and her husband when they flew to Pebble Beach, California, in mid-June on the SunCruz jet to attend the U.S. Open in golf. One week after the open, on June 22, Boulis signed a formal agreement to sell the gambling fleet to Abramoff and Kidan.

In September, at a critical juncture in obtaining outside financing for the deal, Abramoff and Kidan reportedly invited a key executive from Foothill Capital, their lead lender and a subsidiary of Wells Fargo & Co., to Washington to enjoy Abramoff's suite at FedEx Field and take in a football game between the Washington Redskins and the Dallas Cowboys. Greg Walker, the former Foothill executive, told *The Washington Post* in April 2005 that DeLay was in Abramoff's box during the game and that he was briefly introduced to the congressman. A spokesman for DeLay has said that the congressman has no recollection of meeting the executive.

All the wining and dining seemed to help persuade the lenders that Abramoff and Kidan were good risks, even though Kidan's business track record was poor, according to a background check that Foothill Capital had done on him. *The Washington Post* has reported that although Kidan claimed to be worth $26 million, the Foothill credit report about his financial assets indicated that he had been involved in several lawsuits and liens as well as a personal bankruptcy.

Shortly after the football game, a final closing deal with a purchase price of $147.5 million was signed. The terms called for Foothill and another company to lend Abramoff and Kidan $60 million, while Kidan and Abramoff agreed to put up $23 million. In addition, Abramoff and Kidan persuaded Boulis to accept IOUs of $67.5 million. The $23 million that Abramoff and Kidan were obligated to put up to secure their financing was, as they later acknowledged in their guilty pleas, a wire transfer that they had concocted to fool their two lenders into giving them $60 million in loans.

But even after the deal closed in September, there were tensions and disagreements between Kidan and Boulis, who remained as a SunCruz consultant with a 10 percent stake in the casinos. After closing on the deal, Boulis started to balk at some of the terms, and feuding with Kidan intensified: at one point Boulis accused Kidan of having mob ties. The infighting and spats prompted Scanlon to go back to Ney one more time in October of 2000 to seek another statement from him for the *Congressional Record*, which he willingly provided. On October 26, Ney attested to Kidan's stellar business background. Ney declared that since his March statement, "I have come to learn that SunCruz Casino now finds itself under new ownership and, more importantly, that its new owner has a renowned reputation for honesty and integrity. The new owner, Mr. Adam Kidan, is most well known for his successful enterprise, Dial-a-Mattress, but he is also well known as a solid individual and a respected member of the community."

Ney was apparently kept in the dark by Scanlon about Kidan's real résumé, which included the bankruptcy with his Dial-a-Mattress franchise in Washington, plus a recent disbarment from practicing law in New York for alleged fraud involving his mishandling of $100,000 he held in an escrow account for his stepfather. The next year, Ney criticized Scanlon for misleading him about Kidan, and Scanlon told a Florida paper that he was sorry for his actions. According to Abramoff and Scanlon's federal pleas, Ney's second statement in October was followed closely by campaign donations totaling $14,000 that SunCruz and Scanlon made to the National Republican Congressional Committee and to Ney's own campaign committee. Significantly, the contributions to the NRCC had been credited to Ney's name to boost his standing with fellow members.

Abramoff and Kidan as well got a hefty financial boost from the deal. They soon started paying themselves outsize salaries of almost $500,000 a year, and they tapped SunCruz for $310,000 to help underwrite one of Abramoff's sports suites in Washington.

Despite all Ney's exertions and the closing of the deal, the situation at SunCruz remained up in the air and stormy for Abramoff and Kidan. In late November, Abramoff flew to Florida to try to defuse the mounting tensions between the two men, but the mission bought only a little time before the final blowup early in 2001. On his trip, Abramoff met with Boulis and Kidan separately. Abramoff later asserted in court documents that he first heard from Boulis that Kidan had not really provided him the $23 million as the deal required, a statement that was contradicted by other sworn documents signed by Abramoff that he and Kidan had paid Boulis the $23 million.

Infighting with Boulis continued, and at one point in December Kidan claimed that Boulis threatened his life after having attacked him with a pen. Kidan also hired three bodyguards and started to take other safety precautions. Kidan retained a catering and surveillance consultant for SunCruz named Anthony "Fat Tony" Moscatiello, whom federal authorities have linked to the Gambino crime family. Moscatiello, who lived in Howard Beach, New York, has been identified as a bookkeeper for the mob family and a financial adviser to its boss, John Gotti. Kidan and Moscatiello had become acquainted in the early 1990s through the bagel business that Kidan owned on Long Island. As tensions continued to build with Boulis, Kidan also purchased a Mercedes outfitted with armor plating.

Abramoff's dream to get rich through SunCruz was clearly his major, but not his only, preoccupation during 2000. In the midst of all the SunCruz wheeling and dealing, Abramoff was still working at a frantic pace as he juggled lobbying projects and kept up his usual busy schedule of wining and dining members.

In late May, Abramoff managed to mix the two activities by organizing the golf trip to Scotland for DeLay, some of his top staffers, and a few clients that the lobbyist was wooing for more business.

Abramoff helped secure the financing for the trip from some clients and arranged for the National Center for Public Policy Research, where he was a board member, to serve as the official sponsor of the junket as it had done with DeLay's 1997 Moscow trip. This time, much of the cost was borne by two clients, the Choctaws and eLottery. At Abramoff's request, each client had donated $25,000 to the center to finance the trip, which also included a few days of luxury in London.

The ten-day junket, which according to *The Washington Post* cost close to $120,000, featured some high-priced entertainment in London, including tickets to see *The Lion King*, a special request by DeLay and his wife Christine, who also enjoyed lavish accommodations at the Four Seasons Hotel. Besides Abramoff and the DeLays, the trip drew Ed Buckham, who was now a lobbyist; Tony Rudy; and Susan Hirschmann, who had become chief of staff. While they were in Scotland, Abramoff also arranged a dinner party that a couple of lobbyists later likened to the bar scene in *Star Wars* because of Abramoff's diverse array of clients in attendance, including Alexander Koulakovsky, the Russian energy executive, and Terry Martin of the Chitimacha tribe in Louisiana. The setting for the dinner, which also drew some Scottish parliamentarians, took place in an old mansion not far from Edinburgh and the links at St. Andrews, where several of the guests had played a round of golf during the day.

On his official travel forms, DeLay listed the purpose of the trip as educational and noted that he had one meeting in London with former British prime minister Margaret Thatcher. However, when British authorities at the request of U.S. investigators later looked into this meeting, aides to Thatcher described it as a "courtesy call," not a substantive policy discussion. Federal investigators in the Abramoff probe early on made the Scotland trip a part of their inquiry, with an eye on establishing whether the trip entailed any quid pro quos between the lobbyist and DeLay.

Both the Choctaws and eLottery have said they had no idea that their funds were going to pay for the trip but thought they were providing general subsidies for the think tank's operation. The clients weren't the only ones puzzled by the trip's organization. Amy Ridenour, the center's president, who coordinated some of the original logistics with Abramoff, told the Senate committee that because she was about to have a baby she had to give Abramoff the lead in planning and was ultimately surprised to learn of the Scotland leg of the trip.

The outing also proved controversial because Abramoff and Buckham initially picked up thousands of dollars of expenses for the DeLays and some staffers in violation of House rules. Lobbyists are barred from paying for travel for members or staff, even if they're later reimbursed.

But the ten-day junket was a crucial one for Abramoff, who no doubt saw it partly as a business development project, which it proved to be when in September the Chitimacha tribe signed on as a new client. Still more important, the Scotland trip seemed to cement his ties to DeLay Inc. In the weeks following the trip, Rudy and DeLay were to play central parts in killing legislation that was opposed by the two Abramoff clients that helped pay for the junket.

The eLottery fight was a high-stakes one because if the bill, dubbed the Internet Gambling Prohibition Act, had passed, it would have thwarted the ambitions of the gambling services company to sell state lottery tickets on the Internet. DeLay voted in July to kill the bill, despite his longtime stance against gambling and the fact that it was supported by many social and Christian conservatives. The final vote on the bill, which required a two-thirds majority because of a parliamentary rule, pitted 44 GOP members, including DeLay, and 114 Democrats who voted against the bill, while 165 Republicans and 79 Democrats cast yes votes. The bill, which had already passed the Senate, would have made certain kinds of Internet betting a federal crime. DeLay's office has indicated that he voted against the bill because it contained some exemptions for horse and dog racing as well as jai alai.

Rudy, according to e-mails and other documents, worked hand in hand with Abramoff to help orchestrate opposition among House members. According to *The Washington Post*, Rudy assisted Abramoff in large measure by sharing internal congressional communications and offering him strategic advice at critical junctures. Even though DeLay had not stated his position on the Internet gambling legislation in June, Rudy had begun to offer tips to Abramoff that would prove useful in scotching the bill. At one point, Rudy sent an e-mail to Abramoff—revealingly using the words "we should"—in which he urged the lobbyist to contact Paul Weyrich, a powerful Washington conservative who ran the Free Congress Foundation, for help. "I think we should get Weyrich to get like 10 groups to sign a letter to Denny [Hastert] and Armey on gaming bill."

Rudy's role was particularly aggressive and became a focus of federal investigators in part because Abramoff had arranged for Liberty Consulting, a firm that was run by Tony Rudy's wife, Lisa, to receive $25,000 from eLottery. Abramoff had the funds funneled through the conservative nonprofit group Toward Tradition, which was led by Rabbi Daniel Lapin, Abramoff's old friend. Lapin has said that he hired Lisa Rudy on some special projects where he needed outside consulting help.

The eLottery lobbying drive mounted by Abramoff's team

was intense, expensive, and wide-ranging and, before it was over, wound up costing almost $2 million. To defeat the bill, Abramoff also tapped several friends in the evangelical conservative world, including Ralph Reed and the Reverend Louis Sheldon, the head of the Traditional Values Coalition, for their grassroots muscle. Almost $150,000 in eLottery payments to Reed's Century Strategies were channeled through two different groups, one of which was Norquist's Americans for Tax Reform, to mask their true sources and protect the antigambling image of the former evangelical leader. Reed and Sheldon were especially important to the fight because several other prominent conservatives, including Dr. James Dobson, the head of Colorado-based Focus on the Family, were backing the bill and pressuring House GOP members to do likewise.

Despite the eLottery win and picking up new business from the Chitimacha tribe in 2000, the last months of the year were increasingly tense and filled with recriminations as Abramoff and senior lobbyists at the firm clashed on several fronts about older grievances as well as his pursuit of SunCruz during 2000.

One of the firm's other key concerns was Abramoff's interest in foreign representation, which often caused jitters because of his penchant for chasing controversial clients with poor human rights records or other image problems. One arrangement that caused considerable tension had to do with Abramoff's interest in renewing work for Pakistan, which the firm had represented briefly on a single issue in the mid-1990s. Abramoff and Preston Gates had been retained by Pakistan in 1995 and 1996 to help resolve a growing dispute between Washington and Islamabad. Abramoff was trying to help Pakistan obtain American F-16 jets that had been paid for but were being blocked by U.S. sanctions because of concerns about the Pakistani nuclear program, or else get the funds returned.

But Abramoff's lobbying associates generally took a dim view of working for controversial foreign regimes, and not long after the firm's original contract expired, Pakistan increasingly fit that category as it became more radicalized. The prospect of signing Pakistan again was not looked on favorably by most senior members at the firm, and Abramoff only fanned the flames by continuing to pursue more work. At one point, Abramoff even told the other lobbyists that if Pakistan wanted to adopt sharia, Islamic law, that was their choice, and he suggested it shouldn't make a difference in terms of representing the government, a view that shocked others.

Abramoff's far-flung foreign ambitions even extended to business in the Philippines, which he hoped to land with assistance from a powerful but highly controversial friend whose name he dropped with his lobbying associates: Imelda Marcos. Three former colleagues of Abramoff's told me that for a couple of years he used to boast of talking periodically with the legendary wife of the country's former dictator, Ferdinand Marcos. Sources say that Imelda Marcos helped to set up a meeting in Manila in 2000 for Abramoff with then president Joseph Estrada, a former movie star who in 2001 was impeached, forced from office, and charged with corruption. Nothing apparently ever came of Abramoff's business pitch. "There's no question that he was cultivating Mrs. Marcos because he thought he could get something out of it," a former associate of Abramoff's informed me.

Abramoff's foreign escapades caused growing heartburn at Preston Gates. "Jack was traveling more and more and we were knowing less and less about it," a former colleague told me. "There was the overarching question of knowing what Jack was doing." Another former colleague says that from Abramoff's point of view it seemed to be time to move on. "Jack was stifled by the firm," he recalled. "They were trying to rein him in. They were trying to control Jack."

Preston Gates had developed somewhat similar concerns about what Scanlon was up to. After only six months on the job, the firm cashiered Scanlon in part because he wasn't bringing in new clients, as he and Abramoff had promised. Scanlon had been spending much of his time working on projects with Abramoff that the firm was not told much about. "Mike was good at taking an ounce of the truth and turning it into a pound of bullshit," said a former colleague at the firm. When he was terminated, the firm asked Scanlon to return his computer. After a few requests, the computer was sent back looking charred, as though it had been in a fire.

By late 2000, these rifts, coupled with already simmering problems between Abramoff and some top associates over other issues such as the SunCruz deal, led to a major blowup.

In an e-mail Abramoff wrote to himself in November 2000, the lobbyist listed several gripes he had with other associates that underscored just how unhappy Abramoff had become and the depth of the differences with his colleagues. In his e-mail, which was divided into sections that described cultural and financial conflicts, Abramoff wrote that a "chill had descended [on the firm] for at least six months." Abramoff also was very upset over how some senior colleagues regarded his clients, which he thought amounted to treating them as "second class citizens." And Abramoff lamented that the firm wasn't "aggressive enough" in trying to boost revenues and complained that he had "no sense that others are bringing in anything."

Abramoff's e-mail didn't come out of the blue. A few months earlier, Manny Rouvelas, a senior colleague who had long had conflicts with Abramoff over his style and clients, had bluntly warned the lobbyist that he should exercise more caution and slow down. If Abramoff wasn't more "careful," Rouvelas cautioned him, within five years he would find himself "dead, disgraced, or in jail." One former colleague of Abramoff's told me that the frictions between Abramoff and Rouvelas were often intense and had been increasing. "There was definitely a sense that Manny looked down his nose at Jack's clientele." Rouvelas also had suggested to Abramoff that it wasn't a good business model to "just represent a few Indian tribes and a territory."

To be sure, with the election of President George W. Bush that fall, Abramoff's value on K Street for many lobbying firms was palpable, and it didn't take him long to capitalize on it. Not long after he began some quiet negotiations with Greenberg Traurig—a Democratic-leaning firm that seemed to promise him more freedom in chasing controversial clients and fewer restraints in general—Abramoff decided to make the move. By year's end, the lobbyist had cleaned off his desk and was poised to leave with most of his lobbying team and about $6 million a year in business.

FOUR

The Indian Casino Empire

■

As the Bush administration was settling into office in early 2001, Abramoff's lobbying prospects looked rosy, with an all-GOP government affording him a better business landscape. Abramoff moved quickly to exploit the new climate.

Over the next three years, Abramoff's Indian casino business boomed as he signed up several new casino-rich tribes at Greenberg Traurig. His work for tribes such as the Louisiana Coushattas and the Saginaw Chippewas, which signed up in 2001, and the Agua Caliente Band of Cahuilla Indians, which retained Abramoff in 2002, also yielded financial dividends for Abramoff's political allies on Capitol Hill and conservative friends. By mid-2001, Abramoff and Scanlon had launched their covert Gimme Five partnership that led to tens of millions in tribal business going to Capitol Campaign Strategies, the tiny boutique consulting outfit that Scanlon quietly created when Abramoff joined Greenberg Traurig. To Abramoff's dismay, Scanlon was never hired by Greenberg Traurig; he was a consultant for about a year to certain firm clients.

With the Bush administration in power, Abramoff had extra cachet in Washington, and this proved instrumental in his ability to pull in more casino, corporate, and foreign clients. Abramoff could count on help from Ralph Reed and Grover Norquist for access to the White House. Both had long-standing ties with Karl Rove, who also had been acquainted with Abramoff for years through the College Republicans network. Rove, like Abramoff, had once chaired College Republicans.

During the 2000 campaign too, Norquist, and especially Reed, had accumulated more political chits by providing essential help in Southern states such as South Carolina, where they worked during the presidential primaries in the aggressive and expensive effort to knock off Bush's key rival, John McCain. Before the primaries, Reed boasted to some of his colleagues that he would launch a telephone drive against McCain if the Arizona senator emerged as a real threat to Bush. In the South Carolina primary, Reed's Atlanta-based consulting firm Century Strategies fulfilled that pledge. In the wake of McCain's upset victory over Bush in the New Hampshire primary, Reed helped spearhead a direct-mail and telephone drive in South Carolina attacking McCain's conservative bona fides. McCain lost badly in South Carolina, with Bush getting 53 percent of the vote to McCain's 42 percent. Norquist too was involved in helping Bush in early primary states by running issue ads that championed his antitax credentials and disparaged McCain's credentials.

Besides working to build grassroots support for Bush, Reed boosted his standing with the Bush team by raising more than $100,000 for the campaign, making him one of its elite Pioneer fund-raisers. Reed's success was attributable partly to Abramoff, who helped his old friend with some fund-raising contacts and let Reed get the credit with the campaign for certain donations that Abramoff actually raised. In the 2004 campaign, Abramoff would earn Pioneer status too, while Reed would be elevated to Ranger by virtue of raising more than $200,000.

Deepening Abramoff's access, Rove helpfully plucked Susan

Ralston, Abramoff's longtime chief assistant, to play a similar role as gatekeeper in his White House shop. A politically savvy Philippine native, Ralston had become buddies with Reed, who friends say had a role in her getting the White House post with Rove. While Abramoff at first apparently had some mixed feelings about Ralston's departure, he ultimately told associates that he in fact had helped her land the slot, as he quickly divined the upside of Ralston working as a gatekeeper in Rove's office. Abramoff tried to milk these kinds of connections to help his clients with mixed results.

Abramoff's ties to Norquist, though, paid early dividends. In May 2001, Norquist arranged the first of a series of White House visits for state legislators and other backers of the Bush administration's tax-cutting policies. Through Abramoff, Norquist invited some tribal leaders, including Lovelin Poncho of the Coushattas, to the White House to meet the president and have their photos taken with him. Almost simultaneously, both the Coushattas and the Kickapoo tribe of Texas, which also sent a representative to the White House, made $25,000 donations to Norquist's Americans for Tax Reform to back its antitax efforts. Additionally, during certain years some of Abramoff's tribal clients, such as the Coushattas, the Saginaw Chippewas, and a few other tribes, paid about $10,000 to ATR to help underwrite several annual tax policy dinners at Norquist's house that the antitax crusader has long hosted for corporate lobbyists. In exchange for checks, the lobbyists got invited to a handful of dinners a year, where they mingled and discussed issues with high-level administration figures such as Rove and Labor Secretary Elaine Chao plus GOP congressional leaders like DeLay and House Speaker Dennis Hastert.

With Reed's help, Abramoff landed a slot for himself on the transition advisory team for the Interior Department. In that post, Abramoff tried for several months to get friends and allies appointed to top slots—apparently without success—where they would be overseeing policies relating to the Marianas and tribal matters, both of which are under Interior's jurisdiction. In an e-mail to Reed on January 11, 2001, Abramoff wrote, "I was thinking about this appointment [Office of Insular Affairs]. I know it is perhaps a bizarre request, but considering how quickly I was named to the transition advisory team thanks to your request, perhaps it would be possible to ask Karl [Rove] . . . that they should appoint Mark Zachares to head the office of insular affairs . . . Do you think we could get this favor from Karl? It would be my big ask for sure." Reed quickly responded, "It never hurts to ask. What's the next move?" A little later that day Reed followed up with another e-mail: "Just let me know who to call, when to call, and what to say. And while you're at it, get me another client! NOW!" Nothing ever came of their aggressive push to get the job for Zachares, despite the exertions of Abramoff and his lobbying team.

A former lobbying colleague of Abramoff's told me that several other lobbyists were scrambling to get political backing for Zachares, a former secretary of labor on the islands and a close ally of the lobbyist. Abramoff's former associate recalled that about ten letters of support for Zachares were written by members. To push Zachares, Abramoff had a brief meeting with Rove on March 6, but to no avail. The outcome didn't surprise Abramoff's associates, one of whom told me that Zachares was "too radioactive" and had "the worst profile possible" given the political battles in Washington over the islands' treatment of workers. Subsequently, it was revealed that Zachares also had received $10,000 from an Abramoff-run charity, half of which he was given before he held his post in the Marianas government and half of which he got afterward.

Nonetheless, for Greenberg Traurig, Abramoff's arrival and wealth of GOP ties soon translated into an enormous jump in the firm's lobbying earnings. Abramoff was the engine that drove the firm quickly into the top five Washington lobbying firms in terms of revenue. The firm's rise was partly attributable to another Abramoff coup: on his arrival, the lobbyist almost immediately hired Tony Rudy, who had spent a chunk of the previous year working closely and taking expensive junkets with Abramoff while in DeLay's office.

Yet there was one big dark cloud looming over Abramoff, and it soon burst. The situation at SunCruz was about to explode into the news with the brutal gangland-style slaying of Gus Boulis. In the weeks just before the murder, the bad blood between Kidan, the new president of SunCruz, and Boulis had taken a marked turn for the worse.

In late 2000, Kidan had informed Boulis that he was not going to make payments that SunCruz owed him. Kidan then went to court and obtained a restraining order against the former owner, and he also barred Boulis from coming on SunCruz property. In response, on January 19, 2001, Boulis tried to get an injunction to block Kidan from running SunCruz and to compel him to pay him the funds that Boulis claimed he was owed. Events were spinning out of control: on January 31, Kidan also went public with the controversy, telling a Florida paper that Boulis had threatened his life. "I'm not going to sue you, I'm going to kill you," Kidan claimed Boulis had said. "This guy is violent—he's sleazy," Kidan added.

Then on February 6, as Boulis was driving away from his office in downtown Fort Lauderdale at night, his BMW was boxed in by two other cars. One vehicle pulled in front of the BMW, forcing it to stop, while a person in a black Ford Mustang drove alongside the passenger side of Boulis's car and shot him three times. In late September of 2005, three men were arrested and charged with the killing. Two of them, Anthony Moscatiello, sixty-seven, and Anthony Ferrari, forty-eight, had been hired as SunCruz "caterers" and to do "site inspections" and surveillance work by Kidan. The two men had been paid $250,000 for their services to SunCruz, according to legal documents. It's unclear why it took so long to make the arrests, but homicide detectives reportedly had long been probing the payments that were made to the two men in the period right before Boulis's murder. The payments to Moscatiello totaled $145,000, of which $30,000 was sent to his daughter, Jennifer, at her father's request, even though she didn't do any work for SunCruz.

At the time of the killing, Abramoff and Kidan were together in London, but his new colleagues at Greenberg Traurig as well as his old lobbying team were plainly flabbergasted by the news. A few former colleagues of Abramoff's recall a flurry of black humor in the office, with some colleagues joking about whether Abramoff or Kidan could have had anything to do with the Boulis slaying. "Let that be a lesson about crossing us," one of Abramoff's former colleagues quipped to other lobbyists.

No one knew how to respond to the onslaught of press inquiries. Abramoff's fellow lobbyists received word from their boss not to discuss the matter with reporters but to let Scanlon handle the media. Abramoff and Kidan said at the time and have repeated since that they knew nothing about the murder.

Over the next few months, the situation at SunCruz remained in turmoil. Still, Abramoff and Kidan tried to keep their new operation going by looking for more loans and hiring Greenberg Traurig to lobby for them. The two men had ambitious plans: Abramoff was dreaming of expanding the business overseas and was eyeing the Marianas as a possible site. But by spring, the Florida papers had started to write about Kidan's ties to Moscatiello, and the situation was becoming untenable. Soon afterward, the two men were in talks with the Boulis estate and a decision was suddenly made to resolve differences by putting SunCruz into bankruptcy, from which it eventually emerged. As part of the settlement, Abramoff and Kidan transferred most of their financial interest in the company to the estate of Boulis. In exchange, Abramoff and Kidan were released from their liabilities and debts, although this would later be overturned in a bruising court battle with Foothill Capital, their original lender.

Somewhat miraculously, just a few weeks after the killing, it seemed to be business as usual for Abramoff in Washington. One sign of the return to normalcy was a $1,000-a-person fundraiser for Bob Ney that took place in mid-March at Abramoff's box at the Verizon Center (formerly the MCI Center) in Washington, which drew Kidan, Scanlon, and Abramoff.

And even with the ongoing SunCruz drama, Abramoff apparently managed to focus much of his attention in early 2001 on aggressively expanding his Indian casino business.

But the most far-reaching change in Abramoff's lobbying practice was a very well-kept secret. Over the next three years, the scheme that Abramoff and Scanlon had dubbed Gimme Five, their jocular shorthand for kickbacks, would be used by the two men to rake in almost $66 million from six casino-rich tribes. Those funds ostensibly were to pay for Scanlon's public relations and grassroots lobbying services, though almost two-thirds of the total, or $42 million, would be split between Abramoff and Scanlon. Of all their tribal clients, the Coushattas was their biggest score. The tribe paid Abramoff and Scanlon a stunning $32 million for their lobbying and public relations help. The bulk of the funds, close to $27 million, went to Scanlon's Capitol Campaign Strategies or an affiliate, Scanlon Gould Public Affairs.

Essentially, in early 2001, Abramoff started to press hard for his casino clients like the Choctaws and the Coushattas to augment his lobbying work in Washington with much more expensive grassroots campaigns in the states that Scanlon's small consulting firm—which boasted only some half a dozen employees—would ostensibly run. With his Indian clients nervous about losing revenues to other casinos—both in their own states and nearby—Abramoff often hyped various threats to his clients in order to get Scanlon hired at exorbitant rates. Abramoff also hid the salient fact that the majority of the tribal funds that Scanlon's companies received weren't going into radio ads or phone calls or other grassroots techniques, but into the two lobbyists' bank accounts.

In his testimony before the Indian Affairs Committee in 2005, Kevin Sickey, the chairman of the Coushattas, summed up how Abramoff and Scanlon worked their wiles by observing, "They exaggerated political threats and they exaggerated economic threats. Then they exaggerated their ability to deal with these exaggerated threats."

Quite often, the two influence merchants were focused intently on the multimillion-dollar deals they were splitting with each other, and their e-mails descended into a kind of *Animal House* mode of dialogue as they discussed their Gimme Five scams: "Coushatta is an absolute cake walk," Scanlon e-mailed Abramoff about an early payment from the tribe. "Your cut on the project as proposed is at least 800K." To which Abramoff replied, "How can I say this strongly enough: YOU IZ DA MAN."

In early 2001, Abramoff and Scanlon began to plot strategy, sometimes feverishly, it seems, to get their multimillion-dollar kickback partnership under way with Abramoff's new clients, as well as older ones like the Choctaws. In several e-mails released in 2005 by the Indian Affairs Committee, both men joshed with abandon about their Gimme Five plans for the Coushattas and older clients of Abramoff's, like the Choctaws.

The Mississippi tribe, which had long trusted and praised Abramoff for his early work at Preston Gates, was dismayed to learn that about $12 million of the $14.7 million they paid over a three-year period to Scanlon's companies, at Abramoff's urging, was actually divvied up between the two men and pocketed as profits in their scheme. "Don't forget the gimme five aspects," Abramoff e-mailed Scanlon in mid-August 2001 as they were discussing splitting big profits. And on October 17, Abramoff wrote to Scanlon, "So there is more gimme five coming on all these as well, right?"

Donald Kilgore, the attorney general of the Choctaws, in Senate testimony in mid-2005 excoriated Abramoff and Scanlon for their scams. He said that Abramoff and his associates engaged in a "blatant, calculated scheme to defraud a client."

The two Scanlon companies were hardly imposing. Scanlon ran a skeletal operation made up of half a dozen young people in their twenties and a couple of Scanlon's relatives who were on the payrolls. Both Scanlon's sister and mother worked for his firms: his mother helped to make travel arrangements for her son and other employees.

Notwithstanding their modest size, Scanlon's two firms became well known for vastly inflating their real costs to the tribes. Most strikingly, several witnesses at the McCain hearings testified about receiving computerized databases that Scanlon had touted but that in reality involved little new effort. Both the Tiguas and the Saginaw Chippewas pointed out the unusually high price tags that Scanlon charged for his computer databases, which ostensibly contained lists of potential allies, employees, vendors, and others who could be mobilized for letter-writing or phone call efforts. Equally upsetting, Scanlon's much-ballyhooed databases consisted almost entirely of information that the tribes had supplied to him. Moreover, Hisa of the Tiguas told the Indian Affairs Committee that the actual compiling of the customized database was subcontracted by Scanlon's company to another firm.

As the millions poured into Scanlon's companies, both he and Abramoff changed their lifestyles radically, albeit in markedly different ways. Scanlon started to invest in real estate in Rehoboth Beach, where he worked some summers as a life-guard, and elsewhere. He bought two fancy beach houses in Rehoboth, one of which had belonged to the Duponts and cost $4.7 million. He also bought some properties in St. Bart's in the Caribbean and rented an apartment in Washington for $17,000 a month. By contrast, Abramoff used his millions for more personal projects, opening the Eshkol Academy, the Jewish prep school that his two sons attended in suburban Maryland, and an upscale Washington restaurant called Signatures, which in early 2002 had its gala opening. Notwithstanding his financial windfall from the Gimme Five scam, Abramoff seemed to go through his funds at a prodigious pace. In February of 2003, a panicky Abramoff e-mailed Scanlon while he was at his St. Bart's estate: "Mike!!! I need the money TODAY! I AM BOUNCING CHECKS!!!" In response to a Scanlon promise to send him another of his Gimme Five payments, Abramoff calmed down: "Sorry I got nuts, but it's a little crazy for me right now. I am not kidding that I was literally on the verge of collapse. I hate all the s——t I'm into."

The two partners shared other passions. They often played racquetball together and relished exchanging locker room humor. "You better start pulling some real opponents or I am going to beat your ass to a pulp next time we get out there," Scanlon e-mailed Abramoff one day. In turn, Abramoff parried by telling Scanlon that he "was afraid of a real man."

The scam's success at remaining undetected for so long was attributable in good measure to a giant loophole in the lobbying laws that the two influence peddlers deftly exploited. While lobbyists must register for their clients with a congressional office and disclose periodically what they are paid by clients, no similar rules mandated public disclosure of the lucrative fees paid out for the grassroots and public relations work that Scanlon's firm had been set up to handle.

Inflating costs was just one of the tricks Scanlon played on the tribes. Another Scanlon sleight of hand involved creating bogus grassroots groups to generate phone calls, mail, and faxes in support of their casino clients against gaming competitors. In congressional testimony and documents, it was revealed that a significant part of Scanlon's "grassroots" effort involved the use of fictitious groups with clever-sounding names such as the Global Christian Outreach Network, Concerned Citizens Against Gambling Expansion, and Citizens Against Gambling.

This kind of pseudo-grassroots activity was used by Scanlon in a few states, including Michigan and Louisiana, according to documents released by the Senate panel. Scanlon's employees put together phone scripts and messages for these dummy groups, which then were farmed out to consulting firms that specialized in making mass calls on behalf of different clients. Telephone calls then were typically made in the name of these phony antigambling groups to, among others, lists of conservative and religious right supporters, who could in turn be patched through to congressional offices to voice their concerns or send letters.

The underlying rationale for using these kinds of pseudo-outfits to mobilize calls, letters, and faxes from evangelicals and other conservatives was best explained in a revealing Scanlon e-mail: "The wackos get their information through the Christian right, Christian radio, mail, the internet and telephone trees. Simply put, we want to bring out the wackos to vote against something and make sure the rest of the public lets the whole thing slip past them."

Bringing out the "wackos" was a key element of Scanlon's and Abramoff's battle plan to assist tribes in fending off casino rivals. Nowhere, perhaps, did Abramoff and Scanlon find richer turf for these tools than in their work for the Coushattas in Louisiana. Initially, Abramoff and Scanlon stressed the competitive threat to their client from nearby Texas, where they were working with Reed to thwart the Tiguas and the Alabama-Coushattas, who were located near Houston and, being much closer to the Louisiana border, posed a more serious risk. But more important, the Coushattas were fretting about a tiny two-hundred-member tribe in northern Louisiana called the Jena Band of Choctaw Indians, who were eyeing casino opportunities in the state.

Since the Coushattas opened the doors of their Grand Coushatta Casino in Kinder in 1995, it had become one of the most successful Indian gaming ventures nationwide, with revenues of almost $300 million a year. Kinder has the look and feel of a sleepy rural town, with plenty of cows and horses dotting the area's farms and with a population of just two thousand. But the casino is anything but quiet. When I visited in late January 2006, a steady stream of buses, cars, and limousines poured in from nearby Texas cities like Houston and Galveston. The Texas influx also brought in weekly scores of retirees and crowds of younger people.

It's not surprising that the casino has flourished. It offers some thirty-two hundred slot machines—more than the ornate Bellagio in Las Vegas—as well as a wide variety of other games including table poker, blackjack, and much more. There's also a comfortable five-hundred-room hotel and half a dozen restaurants at the complex to cater to the tourist clientele.

The tribe's casino has been an economic boon for the state and is one of the state's largest employers. It's little wonder that the casino has meant good times for the tribe's eight hundred or so members as well. David Sickey, an early critic of Abramoff on the tribe's council, told me that about 60 percent of the casino's revenues go to basic health, education, and welfare programs for the tribe. Tribal members some years receive payments of as much as $60,000 because of the casino's lucrative profits.

Abramoff signed up the Coushattas after his work received a

plug from Terry Martin of the neighboring Chitimachas, who the year before had been on the Scotland golf trip with DeLay. Not long after the outing to Scotland, Martin ran into a couple of top council members for the tribe, William Worfel and Bert Langley, at a conference and praised the lobbyist's work, according to Langley.

A tall, strapping man in his early fifties, Langley became skeptical of Abramoff and Scanlon's high-priced services after a year or so but early on was a backer of theirs. Langley told me that when he first met Abramoff and Scanlon, they boasted of "their friends in Washington and their network." Abramoff also was quick to point out to the Coushattas that Scanlon used to work for DeLay.

When Abramoff and Scanlon were hired in early 2001 by the Coushattas, they had a couple of top priorities. An early project involved helping the tribe obtain a renewal of a formal compact with the state of Louisiana that was needed to keep their casino running. The compact effort had stalled for several months in part because the state had elected a new Republican governor, Mike Foster. A few months after Abramoff and Scanlon started their work, the compact came through, but Langley and others say that it's unclear just how much of a role the two men played in making it happen.

Soon afterward, the two Washington hands shifted gears in their work to block tribal competitors, and according to congressional testimony and records, Scanlon's firm saw a big increase in its business and fees. In 2002 alone, Scanlon's firm took in almost $12 million from the tribe.

The major lobbying missions that Abramoff and Scanlon undertook for the tribe focused on thwarting business rivals—both Indian and nontribal gambling enterprises—that might cut into their revenues. While the Coushattas faced some real competitive threats, Abramoff and Scanlon sometimes hyped other dangers to ensure that their workload and fees would keep growing, say Coushatta tribal members. Several Coushatta council members told me that they attribute the ability of Abramoff and Scanlon to get so much for their services in part to the inexperience and gullibility of two top leaders at the time—Coushatta chief Lovelin Poncho, and his deputy, William Worfel. "Abramoff could stroke Worfel's ego," David Sickey told me. "He played Worfel like a fiddle. It emboldened Abramoff. He manipulated the internal tribal leadership."

The Coushattas turned into a gravy train not just for Abramoff and Scanlon but also for a wider circle of conservative political allies. Above all, the Coushatta lobbying drive underscored the importance that Abramoff attached to deploying Ralph Reed in state battles to build alliances with social conservatives who would help his gambling clients. Just as Reed did in Texas in 2001, where he mobilized his religious right comrades to help shut down the Tiguas' casino, the ex–evangelical leader sought out old friends from his days at the Christian Coalition, such as Dr. James Dobson, for help in Louisiana. In all these campaigns, Reed and Abramoff quietly worked out deals so that conduits could sanitize Reed's payments. Much of the money, some $2.3 million, flowed from the Coushattas and the Choctaws through the Scanlon-run American International Center in Rehoboth Beach, before it was sent to Reed's Century Strategies in Duluth, Georgia. Other monies for Reed were routed through Scanlon's Capitol Campaign Strategies. During the Indian Affairs Committee hearings, the different covers that Reed used were slowly peeled back. In one hearing in mid-2005, Worfel testified that the "payments were made to Ralph Reed" by the tribe. When pressed about whether Reed understood where the money was coming from, Worfel responded, "I don't want to speculate, but he should know."

Reed's initial mission in Louisiana in early 2001 was to

thwart a bill that would have eased state restrictions on riverboat gambling, a potential financial threat to the Coushattas' bottom line. Early on, Reed turned to Tony Perkins, a key state legislator and champion of social conservative causes who later moved to Washington to run the Family Research Council, a powerful conservative advocacy group. Perkins, whom Reed hailed as the "antigambling leader" in the state, lobbied his fellow legislators against the riverboat bill and encouraged Reed to do a radio blitz and other actions as well. Reed also called on Jerry Falwell, the former leader of the Moral Majority, who was kind enough to do a phone message opposing the legislation.

In addition, Reed convinced his old boss, Pat Robertson, founder of the Christian Coalition, to provide a message of support. Reed wrote to Robertson in late March 2001 that he was working on "behalf of pro family groups in Louisiana" and was hoping that Robertson might aid the cause too. After Robertson weighed in with a message, Reed shot him a quick thank-you for his "leadership for our values." Nonetheless, there is no evidence that Reed's religious allies in the campaign knew that the Coushattas were underwriting Reed's work. Reed's efforts paid off in mid-2001, when the bill that would have eased the curbs on riverboat gambling went down to defeat—much to the advantage of the Coushattas' casino business.

But this fight was just a harbinger of a much bigger lobbying blitz that was to come against other competitors. The bulk of team Abramoff's lobbying was aimed at blocking the very poor Jena Band tribe, which lacked a reservation but wanted to open their own casino not far from where the Coushattas' casino was headquartered. The battle to block the Jenas soon became a multifront war: Abramoff and Scanlon worked to create political pressures against the Jenas in Louisiana as well as in Washington, where the Interior Department was for two years bombarded with mail, phone calls, personal lobbying by Abramoff and his allies, letters from members of Congress, and much more. The anti-Jena drive turned into a seesaw battle that stretched over two years. In 2002, Abramoff and his allies won a victory at Interior, but in 2003 it was reversed when the department approved a revised casino project for the Jenas.

Inside Washington, Abramoff tapped Italia Federici, a little-known conservative activist whom he had met through Norquist, for her pull at Gale Norton's Department of the Interior. Federici ran the Council of Republicans for Environmental Advocacy, an Orwellian-sounding organization that was mostly funded by energy interests, including mining and oil giants. The group spent much of its energy blasting environmental groups. CREA had been started in 1997 by Norquist and Gale Norton, when she was attorney general in Colorado. Federici, who also had lived in Colorado before moving to Washington, had met Norton—a protégé of James Watt, the disgraced Interior secretary under Reagan—while working on one of her political campaigns.

The ties that Abramoff forged with the council were based heavily on tribal largesse: over a few years, Federici told the Senate Indian Affairs Committee, she received almost half a million dollars from Abramoff's tribal clients, a sum that was roughly equal to her annual budget for two years. The Coushattas were the most generous of Abramoff's tribal donors, chipping in $150,000 in two installments to CREA's coffers. The other large tribal donor was the Saginaw Chippewas, who donated one check for $75,000.

Abramoff found Federici useful not only because she knew Norton but because of other ties too. Lobbyists and government sources have said that she had a close personal tie to J. Steven Griles, the number-two official in the department, who had previously been a well-paid energy lobbyist on K Street.

Abramoff's courtship of Federici intensified in 2001. In late

September, Abramoff received an irresistible invitation from Federici that allowed him to boost the tribe's profile and contacts. She had organized an intimate dinner party in Georgetown at the home of Julie Finley, a wealthy GOP fund-raiser, which was billed as a tribute to Secretary Norton. The event, which drew some two dozen guests, included Abramoff, Griles, and Lovelin Poncho, the chairman of the Coushattas, who came to town for the occasion.

The next day in an e-mail to Federici, Abramoff described himself as "jazzed" and seemed ecstatic about the party. "The event last night was outstanding," he wrote. "Bravo . . . I have a fantastic box at the Redskins stadium. How about you come this Sunday and see it (invite Steve to come with his family too) and we'll all discuss my doing a fundraiser for you guys? Let me know as soon as you can . . . I think Attorney General John Ashcroft and his guys will also be there."

Shortly after the CREA dinner with Abramoff and his Coushatta client, Federici responded with an inquiry about whether Abramoff could speed up some requests for funding. "Ahhh—the glamorous world of non profit work—about one half step above beggar." Besides discussing money matters with Federici, Abramoff often referred in his e-mails to "our guy Steve" and cited the importance of CREA as "our access to Norton." A former colleague of Abramoff's recalls being told that the group was "important for dealings with the Department of the Interior."

The Federici contacts seemed to prove helpful to Abramoff when in early 2002 the Jena battle began in earnest. The fight was sparked when the tribe surprised the Coushattas and Abramoff by getting an okay from Governor Foster of Louisiana to open a casino in Vinton, just an hour's drive from the Coushattas.

The next step for the Jenas was to get the necessary regulatory approval in early 2002 from the Department of Interior, and that's where Abramoff and his team mobilized for a knock-down, drag-out fight. The time window to block action by Interior was only forty-five days and Abramoff had to hurry. The lobbyist turned to allies inside and outside Washington to wage a fast and expensive full-court press.

Abramoff's team asked their allies to increase pressure on Interior officials and members of Congress, particularly key ones from Louisiana and nearby Mississippi, where the Mississippi Choctaws also viewed a Jena casino as an economic threat.

Early on in the fight, Abramoff faxed a quick message to Griles asking for his help in setting up a meeting between Chief Martin of the Choctaws and Norton. Griles responded by forwarding a message on the subject to Norton's assistant. Griles reminded Norton that Chief Martin had not been at the CREA dinner that Federici threw for the Interior secretary in September 2001 and added, "Need let Jack know if this can happen!" Not long after Abramoff's e-mail to Griles, Chief Martin was invited to Interior on February 5, where he had separate meetings with Griles and Norton.

On a second track, Abramoff and Scanlon again activated Ralph Reed, who in turn reached out to his allies on the Christian right such as Dobson, the leader of Colorado-based Focus on the Family whose daily radio show attracts millions of listeners. The move to deploy Dobson's group seems to have been especially adroit because of Norton's Colorado background.

Tom Minnery, a key aide to Dobson, weighed in with a letter to Norton opposing the Jenas and stressed that the state already had an "alarming number of gaming establishments." To drive home his message, Minnery forwarded a copy to White House chief of staff Andrew Card. Michael Rossetti, a former counselor to Norton at Interior, told me that the involvement of Dobson's group "really scared Interior officials." Rossetti added that

Dobson was seen as someone who could quickly flood Interior with a tidal wave of calls that "could shut our phone lines." In an e-mail that Abramoff sent to Scanlon on February, 20, 2002, the lobbyist gloated that "Reed may finally have scored for us! Dobson goes up on the radio on this next week."

Meanwhile Abramoff was scrambling for more help on Capitol Hill and found an ally in Representative David Vitter. A Louisiana Republican, Vitter wrote to Norton opposing the Jena casino project and later organized more than two dozen members of the House to sign a another letter to Norton—right before the March 7 deadline—that carried a similar message. Finally, the lobbyist in early March sent his tribal client a long list of more than five dozen suggested political contributions, many of which were approved. High on the list was a proposal to send $100,000 to Federici's group, which, according to tribal records, was done on March 6, 2002.

The very next day, Interior ruled against the Jena request for a compact in the state. Interior spokesman Dan DuBray strongly rejected any suggestion that the decision "was influenced by any kind of outside pressure." DuBray added that the decision was reached after the required review of forty-five days on the basis that the Jena compact didn't meet Interior standards.

The Jenas didn't accept defeat. Later in the year and during 2003, the tribe mounted a new drive to secure Interior approval for a casino at a different location, in Logansport, Louisiana. To bolster their case, the Jenas also hired more lobbyists, including a former aide to Rep. Billy Tauzin of Louisiana, and slowly their new casino plan appeared to be winning converts at Interior.

To help squelch the new challenge, Abramoff and his team again turned up pressure on Hill allies and pushed Federici to use her contacts at Interior. In June 2003, Abramoff pulled off something of a coup by getting all four House leaders—including DeLay and Speaker Dennis Hastert—to sign a letter to Norton opposing the Jena project. The leaders criticized the proposed casino plan on the grounds that the site selected wasn't on their reservation and entailed "reservation shopping," a practice that's sometimes done to obtain a casino license.

It's unclear whether DeLay or Hastert took the lead in circulating this letter. But the letter drew extra attention afterward when it was reported that it was sent in close proximity to a big fund-raiser for the speaker at Abramoff's restaurant. On June 3, 2003, just a week before the letter was sent to Norton, a bash at Signatures pulled in some $21,500 from Abramoff's firm and his tribal clients for Keep Our Majority (KOMPAC), the speaker's PAC. Hastert has denied that the fund-raiser had any connection to the anti-Jena missive.

Still, the effort also raised eyebrows with some tribal lobbyists in Washington, because it was rare to have four House leaders, so removed from a state fight like the one in Louisiana, team up on such a joint letter. "It was very unusual to see four House leaders weigh in on any Indian issue, let alone one that on its face involved only a small poor tribe in Louisiana," Heather Sibbison, a lobbyist at Patton Boggs who represented the Jenas, told me.

Other members also wrote letters to back Abramoff and his client. Abramoff's team reached out to several senior Republican members they had good ties with, such as John Doolittle of California, Pete Sessions of Texas, and Dana Rohrabacher of California. Several letters also came from Democrats, including Senator Harry Reid of Nevada and Senator Byron Dorgan of North Dakota; these were generated by some of Abramoff's Democratic associates at Greenberg Traurig.

Meanwhile, Abramoff had prodded Federici to again try to push Griles to intervene in the matter. In an e-mail in early December 2002, Abramoff raised the specter of another Jena drive and asked for her help. "It seems that the Jenas are on the march again. If you can, can you make sure that Steve squelches this again? Thanks!!" Federici answered, "Thanks for the update. I'll bring it up asap."

Other e-mails also underscored the symbiotic ties between Abramoff and Federici. At one point in early April 2003, Abramoff e-mailed Federici an "urgent alert" about an impending policy shift at Interior, a reference to a potentially different stance on the Jena casino. "Any way to see if this is something coming from the top," he queried on April 3. Federici offered to "see what I can find out," but added, "I hate to bug you, but is there any news about a possible contribution . . ."

The Indian Affairs panel probed into these links aggressively in late 2005 at one of their hearings. It was a testy and combative session. When Federici was asked about the heavy e-mail traffic between Abramoff and herself, she replied, "We work with people every day with varying levels of decorum." But Federici gamely downplayed her ties with the lobbyist. Abramoff, she conceded, "did ask me for assistance, but it was not the body of the work I did." And Federici insisted that she was merely "responding to Jack as a friend, as I would respond to any friend who had a need or question."

These kinds of responses prompted more sharp questions from Senator McCain, who warned Federici more than once to answer questions or face possible contempt charges. At one point, a frustrated McCain commented acidly to Federici, "That's a remarkable answer." Other panel members were also skeptical. "I come from a pretty small town, but I think I can spot a pretty big lie," Senator Byron Dorgan, the panel's ranking Democrat, angrily quipped. "I am not lying to this committee," she shot back.

Despite all her disclaimers, Abramoff seemed to think highly of Federici's help. "Unfortunately she is critical to me," he confided to a lobbying associate in an e-mail. The Abramoff e-mails were also buttressed by Senate testimony of Norton's former aide, Michael Rossetti, who indicated his strong worries about Griles's involvement in the issue. Rossetti later confirmed to me his deep concerns about Griles's unusual—and possibly inappropriate—interest in the Louisiana fight. "Griles was pushing unusually hard and repeatedly to participate in a meeting with the secretary about the Jenas where a decision would be made," he recalled. During the same period, Griles also inexplicably handed Rossetti a binder of materials critical of the Jenas' proposal. When pressed about its origins, Griles conceded to Rossetti it had most likely been the handiwork of Abramoff's team.

Apparently, Abramoff pulled out all the stops to obtain help from Griles. At one point in September 2003, Griles dined in Washington with Abramoff and Fred Baggett, the chairman of Greenberg Traurig's government affairs practice. At the dinner, Griles told the Senate panel, Abramoff surprised him by making him a job offer, because the department was in the midst of making a decision on the Jenas' second proposal.

When Griles was questioned by the Senate panel about the propriety of such a meeting and discussion, he testified that the offer "raised alarms with me." Griles said that the next day he went to ethics officials at Interior to alert them to the offer in order to avoid any charges of conflict of interest. What's more, Griles downplayed his role in the Jena fight, testifying that he had met Abramoff only once or twice and didn't treat him any differently from other lobbyists.

Both Griles and Federici have reportedly been under scrutiny by the federal criminal task force probing Abramoff's influence-peddling operations in Washington, but both have insisted that they did nothing improper.

At the end of 2003, however, despite all Federici's efforts and the congressional pressure that Abramoff brought to bear on Interior in 2003, Norton sided with the Jenas and dealt the Coushattas a big setback. For the Coushattas, the impact of Interior's decision was intensified by the increasing concern of some council members about the huge fees that Abramoff and Scanlon had charged them. At the Senate hearing, two brothers from the Coushattas, David and Kevin Sickey, both of whom were leading tribal critics of Abramoff and Scanlon, presented eloquent critiques of the lobbyist's work. Kevin Sickey, who had taken over as the tribe's chairman after a bitter internal fight about the huge lobbying costs, described the heavy fallout for the Coushattas and other tribes from their experience with the two influence merchants.

"Jack Abramoff is not a product of Indian Country," Sickey told the panel in late 2005. "On the contrary, he is the golden boy gone bad of the American political system. Our tribe and others were victimized when we attempted to fit into the American political system and we were led to believe that Abramoff was the gatekeeper."

FIVE

The Fix

■

In the fall of 2001, an obscure election for seats on a tribal council in Michigan made Scanlon and Abramoff deliriously happy. The two influence merchants had been fighting an uphill and seemingly futile battle for most of the year to get the business of the Saginaw Chippewas. But they had been foiled by a recalcitrant group of tribal council members who didn't want to hire them in part because of concerns about costs. Finally, Abramoff and Scanlon hit on a novel plan of attack to convince the tribe to retain them.

In a highly controversial ploy to win business from the tribe, Abramoff and Scanlon made moves to meddle in a tribal council election—a potential violation of the Indian Civil Rights Act of 1968. The goal was to put enough of their allies on the tribal council so that they could then be hired. In the run-up to the elections, brochures and flyers were printed up and distributed by Scanlon and his allies on the tribe, a campaign that cost close to $100,000, according to congressional testimony and documents. The campaign materials they disseminated backed the election of a small group running for the tribal council that they called the "slate of eight," some of whom had indicated their support for hiring Abramoff and Scanlon.

In the pre-election machinations, Scanlon and Abramoff appear to have received help from Chris Petras, the tribe's legislative director, who, though not a Chippewa himself, seems to have been an early ally of theirs. Abramoff sent one e-mail to Scanlon not long before the election in which he remarked on Petras's enthusiastic response to an expensive multimillion-dollar lobbying campaign that Abramoff had outlined. "I had dinner with Chris Petras tonight of the Sag Chip. He was salivating at the $4 to $5 million program I described to him. He's going to come in after the primary with the guy who will be chief if they win (a big fan of ours already) and we are going to help him win. If he wins, they take over in January, and we make millions."

Immediately following the November 2001 tribal elections, Scanlon wrote an ecstatic memo to Abramoff and his other colleagues in the effort. "Well team . . . Last night was amazing—the slate of 8 kicked ass; and I want to thank all of you for helping out—and watching the bottom line." Scanlon noted that seven out of the eight candidates they were trying to elect had won and added that, "Maynard will be elected chief at the organizational meeting on December 4th and hopefully we'll be doing some more work for the tribe in the near future." Abramoff replied: "I love it."

Some of these allies had been courted aggressively by Abramoff and Scanlon prior to the elections. Petras appears to have been one of a few friends who periodically received gifts from Abramoff, according to documents released by the Senate committee. In an e-mail that was sent to Abramoff on December 12, 2000, by Susan Ralston, Abramoff's top assistant at the time, Petras was on a gift list to receive $200 at the end of the year. Two tribal members were also listed for similar gifts: David

Otto and chief Phillip Peters, who was soon to be replaced by Maynard Kahgegab, Jr. Both Otto and Kahgegab were among the victorious candidates in the slate of eight.

At a Senate Indian Affairs hearing in the fall of 2004, Petras was asked if he ever received any gifts from Abramoff and Scanlon. He ticked off a few items: a digital camera, a leather travel documents holder, and a slide projection desktop screen. Asked if he thought this was proper or improper, Petras said, "It was at Christmas time." Petras denied repeatedly that he'd had any role in their election campaign effort, though some of the Scanlon and Abramoff e-mails suggest otherwise.

Once the new council and chief were in place in late 2001, the contracts that the duo had been seeking came through after several months, though not quite fast enough to satisfy Scanlon and Abramoff. In a series of e-mails on December 17, Abramoff and Scanlon first seemed ebullient that their ship had come in and then revealed disappointment at the tribe's delays in making decisions.

"Just spoke with Chris," Abramoff e-mailed Scanlon. "Chris said they are voting on the project today!! Can you smell money????"

Scanlon replied a little later: "Did we win it?"

Abramoff in turn wrote: "The f' troglodytes didn't vote on you today. Dammit."

"What's a troglodyte?" Scanlon queried.

"What am I, a dictionary? . . . It's a lower form of existence basically."

Soon afterward, though, the details were ironed out and contracts were inked. Abramoff and Greenberg Traurig were hired to do Washington lobbying at a fee of $150,000 a month, almost fifteen times higher than the previous lobbyist, a Democrat named Larry Rosenthal, had been paid.

But more significantly, Abramoff persuaded the Chippewas to sign a much bigger deal for Scanlon's services without telling the tribe that there was any kind of formal business or financial tie between them. Not long after he started working for the Chippewas in 2002, Scanlon pushed hard to get financing for a project—similar to ones he did for the Tiguas and other tribes—that involved creating a database of Michigan voters and allies to use in political fights against rival gaming projects. The price tag for the database was $4.5 million, a fee that other industry consultants regarded as outrageous. The cost raised eyebrows and prompted critical questions from some council members who worried about just what they were getting for all that money. An early and persistent critic of the high bills was Bernie Sprague, the subchief of the Chippewas, who fought hard for more scrutiny of the lobbyists.

A strong-looking man in his late forties with a friendly but slightly wary demeanor, Sprague quickly became a leading critic of Abramoff and Scanlon. In his congressional testimony before the Indian Affairs panel in the fall of 2004, Sprague said that the tribal council later researched the database and found they could purchase a database of every Michigan voter for $75,000. "This type of spending was repeated over and over and over again, costing our tribe over $14 million."

More broadly, Sprague pointed out in his testimony that in the elections in late 2001 that led to the hiring of Abramoff and Scanlon, the two men had "smeared the reputations of other candidates running for tribal council," which was crucial to getting most of their favored "slate of eight" into office.

Even after the scandal broke, Sprague remained angry about how the two Washington influence merchants had manipulated their elections and leaders to win business. "These guys were professional con artists," he told me during a two-day visit I made to the tribe in the fall of 2005. "They were looking for vulnerable tribal leaders who were looking for power."

In the wake of the 2001 tribal elections, Abramoff and Scanlon found both with the new council. They also found another lucrative casino to further enrich themselves. About an hour's drive north of the state capital of Lansing, the Chippewas' Soaring Eagle Casino and Resort complex is located a couple of miles from downtown Mount Pleasant, the home of Central Michigan University. Besides its flourishing casino, which brings in an estimated $400 million a year, Soaring Eagle boasts a hotel with 514 guest rooms that is handsomely decorated with Indian artifacts and motifs. The hotel seems to have done a good job in attracting professional groups from around the state for conventions. When I visited, a few conventions were under way, including two for state medical organizations.

Like the Coushattas and the Tiguas, the tribe has also used a large percentage of its casino revenues to fund a wide variety of health and education programs to benefit the tribe's thirty-two hundred members. Since it opened for business in 1998, the casino has provided annual payments to adult Chippewas that in 2005 came to an estimated $70,000 per person.

Sprague's uphill battle to get Scanlon and Abramoff ousted shows just how far the schemers would go to intimidate and quash any critics of their work. Sprague speaks calmly and with a dry sense of humor and a strong sense of outrage about how the two Washington lobbyists manipulated some members of the tribe to get what they wanted. He told me that he once spoke to other council members about his concerns that Abramoff had been embroiled in the SunCruz controversy and had also noted that the previous owner had been killed. Soon after he began to voice his skepticism, Sprague heard rumblings that Abramoff was considering bringing a libel suit against him, and he decided to talk directly to the lobbyist. When Sprague reached him by phone one day, Abramoff initially charged that Sprague was telling other council members that the lobbyist had been involved in the murder of Boulis. "He said I was spreading

rumors that he had somebody killed in Florida," Sprague recalled. "Abramoff said he had a reputation to protect."

But Sprague calmly informed Abramoff that he had said
nothing of the kind; all he'd done was mention to other council
members that SunCruz seemed to be a big headache and that
Boulis had been killed. Abramoff backed down after their con-
versation. But Sprague's brief phone encounter with Abramoff
was just a taste of what happened in the next year or so as he
raised substantive questions with tribal council members about
the work of the two Washington hands.

Repeatedly, Sprague found that requests for information
about what Abramoff and Scanlon actually did for the tribe and
the high costs of their work were rebuffed by their allies on the
council. When Sprague and one or two other dissidents on the
council asked to talk directly to Abramoff and Scanlon, they
were usually informed that they were too busy. Finally, at one
point in 2003, Sprague was told bluntly by a strong Abramoff
backer on the council "not to mess with the big dogs," if he
knew what was good for him. In apparent retaliation for his ongoing criticism of the Washington lobbyists, Sprague told me
that his longtime job as parks and recreation commissioner was
eliminated. He remained out of work for almost six months.

Sprague isn't the only council member who ran into flak by
raising tough questions. Audrey Falcon, the onetime nurse who
was elected tribal chief in late 2003, told me that when she and
Sprague once pressed Scanlon for documentation about an invoice the tribe had received for $1.2 million, he wasn't able to
explain it. "Scanlon came but never brought any report," Falcon
recalled. "He seemed defensive and didn't want to tell us much.
Nobody really trusted him." Falcon and Sprague both told me
that they had also asked Abramoff, at one point, if he and Scanlon had any formal business relationship, and Abramoff had denied any financial ties with the PR consultant.

To be sure, Abramoff and his lobbying team did score some wins for the tribe in the area of appropriations. But perhaps the largest win, a $3 million grant from the Bureau of Indian Affairs for a Chippewa school, quickly became a political hot potato for the tribe and for Senator Conrad Burns of Montana, the powerful Republican chairman of a Senate appropriations subcommittee that funds Interior and its Bureau of Indian Affairs, who pushed hard for the $3 million. The effort was controversial because the school construction grants are intended for poorer tribes with run-down schools, and the Chippewas, awash with casino revenues, didn't fall in that category under BIA guidelines.

Abramoff, who boasted to *Vanity Fair* that "every appropriation we wanted from [Senator Burns' committee] we got," had several close ties to Burns. Over a five-year period, Burns received just over $141,000 from the lobbyist and his tribal clients, more than any other member of Congress. Abramoff's team also included two former Burns staffers as lobbyists at different times. The first hire from Burns's office was Shawn Vasell, who joined Abramoff at Preston Gates and then returned to the Hill for a couple of years before coming back and rejoining the lobbyist at Greenberg Traurig. "Our staffs were as close as they could be," Abramoff told *Vanity Fair*. "They practically used Signatures as their cafeteria."

The $3 million grant was secured through a so-called earmark, one of the lobbyist's favorite tools for getting what he wanted without attracting public attention. In late 2003, without public debate or notice, Burns placed an earmark into a final appropriations bill just before it was going to be voted on. Burns's contribution, which lifted prior curbs on funds going to the Chippewa school, was only a paragraph long and was inserted at the last minute into a conference report.

A month after Burns's earmark, the Chippewas gave $4,000

to Burns's campaign committee, and two months later the senator's chief of staff, Will Brooke, joined Abramoff as lobbyist. Abramoff had actually been cultivating Brooke for some time. In early 2001, Brooke was one of a few staffers who were invited to the Super Bowl and flew down for a night of entertainment, including some gambling on a SunCruz ship near Miami. Brooke, in early 2006, told a Montana paper that he was voluntarily cooperating with the Justice Department probe into Abramoff's influence peddling.

Ironically, the Chippewas had one of the better schools in Indian country, and subsequently several council members indicated embarrassment about the grant. They were also concerned because Abramoff had engineered the earmark in such a way that after the $3 million in construction funding, the tribe would have to come up with millions more to cover operational costs. Burns said he acted not at Abramoff's behest but because two Democratic senators from Michigan had asked for his help with the matter.

Not surprisingly, the $3 million grant to the Chippewas didn't sit well with Indian tribes in Montana; a few of whom had tried unsuccessfully to get Burns's help for local projects. One of the state's larger tribes, the Blackfeet, was particularly irked to learn of the senator's efforts to help a tribe in Michigan.

Carol Juneau, a representative in the Montana legislature for the Blackfeet Reservation, and other members of the tribe have voiced dismay about Burns's failure to look after local tribes. In interviews with National Public Radio, Juneau said that when she learned of Burns's help for the Chippewas she thought "he forgot where he came from." Juneau and others from Montana also have pointed out that the Chippewas are much wealthier than the Blackfeet because of their gambling revenues. Betty Cooper, a member of the Blackfeet tribal council, told NPR too that the local tribe had a much greater need for school funds, observing that Montana's school facilities are dangerously run-down, putting school kids at risk. "We were next on the list to get our facility when he put this money to this Michigan tribe." Cooper recounted that the tribe went to Burns a few years before the Chippewas got their grant but never received any help from the senator. Cooper concluded that all the campaign funds that Burns received from Abramoff and his clients had favorably inclined him to help the lobbyist's client before his own constituents.

Burns, whose ties to Abramoff became a campaign issue for him early in the 2006 elections, continued to defend his actions and stressed that Abramoff and Scanlon had nothing to do with his effort to help the tribe. But the federal task force looking into Abramoff's wide-ranging influence-peddling operation was scrutinizing Burns's role and that of his aides in pushing the earmark despite the concerns of BIA officials about the grant's propriety.

Eventually, the $3 million grant became too much of a political embarrassment and a liability for the Chippewa tribe too. In April 2006, the tribal council notified Burns and Congress in a letter that they wanted the funds, which still had not been released, to be used instead to offset cuts in the BIA's budget. The tribe's letter concluded that it wasn't "financially prudent to pursue this project at this time."

The Chippewas' decision wasn't easy, but it was one that the tribe's leaders hoped would help put the political and financial headaches left by Abramoff and Scanlon behind them. Yet their legacy is a hard one to forget for many members of the Michigan tribe. "Even though Abramoff is gone, we're still dealing with him," Falcon said with a pained expression. "We're still dealing with the fallout." Sprague too remains upset: "They created the scam and went out and chose their prey," he told me on a sunny fall day in 2005. "We weren't the only tribe to be taken advantage of."

Indeed, Abramoff and Scanlon also were hired after spending large sums on candidates in a tribal election in early 2002 in California, involving the Agua Caliente tribe of Cahuilla Indians. The Palm Springs–based tribe retained Abramoff and Scanlon in mid-2002, shortly after two new council members were elected, giving pro-Abramoff forces a slim three-to-two majority. Richard Milanovich, the chairman of the tribe, who opposed the hiring of Abramoff and Scanlon, testified at the first hearing of the Senate panel in the fall of 2004 about his early concerns. Milanovich told the committee that he had learned that Scanlon and Abramoff had entered into a "secret cabal with certain tribal members" to whom "assistance" was provided in order to get themselves hired.

The Agua Caliente elections in March 2002 were intensely worked beforehand by Scanlon and Abramoff. In one e-mail not long before the elections, Scanlon queried, "How much do you want me to spend on the AC race—I gotta get a team out there ASAP—Then rotate a new team in after that—So travel is gonna run about 20K and materials like 5–10K. Should we go for it?" Without hesitation, Abramoff answered, "Yes go for it big time."

In late February 2002, Abramoff had a meeting with some supporters in the tribe and, judging by an e-mail he sent Scanlon, seemed upbeat about their prospects. Abramoff wrote Scanlon that he'd just met with a backer of theirs and they "can't wait for you to lead them into the promised land."

As part of the effort to take the tribe into "the promised land," Scanlon developed talking points and a "message" for their candidates that read at times like psychobabble. "We will communicate that this election is about direct leadership with leaders who are in touch with the tribe. You are the new leaders, the leaders who will take the tribe into the future. Not the old leaders who are looking out for number one."

After the elections, the balance on the council shifted, and Milanovich and the number two were in a minority. In July of 2002, the tribe signed separate contracts with Greenberg Traurig and Scanlon Gould Public Affairs, which together cost the tribe just under $10 million for a year and a half of work.

One of the major projects that Scanlon undertook for the tribe soon came under fire because of its exceedingly high costs. In an effort to pressure then California governor Gray Davis to let the tribe have more slot machines, Scanlon launched a letter-writing campaign that turned into a financial fiasco. By the time it was completed, the tribe's bill from Scanlon totaled $7.4 million, but only two thousand letters were generated—which translated into about $3,700 per letter.

These and other problems caused tribal complaints to increase and prompted Abramoff in an e-mail to counsel Scanlon not to take their critics too seriously. "I think the key thing to remember with all these clients is that they are annoying, but the annoying losers are the only ones that have this kind of money and part with it so quickly."

Long after the scandal began, Milanovich felt vindicated in his concerns about Abramoff and Scanlon, but he remained embittered and deeply embarrassed about the repercussions for many tribes. "It really pains me," Milanovich told a gathering of tribal leaders in January 2006. "It hurts me to know the fallout that is affecting all of Indian country."

SIX

The Influence Machine

■

On a mid-February night in 2002, Abramoff's stock in Washington skyrocketed. The opening of his restaurant, Signatures, at 801 Pennsylvania Avenue, NW, was a gala event, packed with friends from Capitol Hill, the Bush administration, and K Street. Mingling in the crowd that evening were close ideological allies and friends such as Dana Rohrabacher and Tom DeLay, as well as dozens of GOP aides from several leadership offices, and a small army of lobbyists. Also making appearances that night were some Bush administration friends such as White House political guru Karl Rove and Press Secretary Ari Fleischer.

Abramoff was close to the peak of his influence when the restaurant opened. From his favorite corner perch at table forty, Abramoff could talk quietly with GOP friends and conservative allies about issues of mutual concern—fund-raising, lobbying, golf junkets, and more. Over the next two years, the restaurant hosted dozens of fund-raisers for members. There was reportedly a "comp list" for special friends such as DeLay, Bob Ney, and Rohrabacher, who could enjoy food and drink on the house. Ney was well known as a regular at Abramoff's eatery, sometimes showing up two or three times a week and spending hours there with some of his young staff and other friends from the lobbying world.

The walls of Signatures were decorated with historic documents. One prominent display was a replica of President Gerald Ford's signed pardon for Richard Nixon, which sold for $5,000. Elsewhere in the restaurant, there were signed photos or letters of Harry Houdini, General George Patton, and gangster Meyer Lansky, all of which were for sale. The entrees, which tended to be pricey and drew decidedly mixed reviews, featured $74 Kobe beef and several kinds of sushi that were favorites of Abramoff, Scanlon, and Rudy. For good measure, the restaurant prepared kosher meals for Abramoff. The ads for Signatures, appropriately enough, boasted that it served "liberal portions in a conservative setting." The opening of Signatures elevated Abramoff into an elite circle of lobbyists who were restaurant entrepreneurs, such as Democratic rival Tommy Boggs and GOP star Haley Barbour, who were co-owners of the Caucus Room, another power restaurant in the capital.

Signatures was the latest addition to the lobbyist's far-flung influence-peddling empire that his Indian casino clients and others—including the Marianas and Russian energy interests— were instrumental in underwriting. His political leverage too was enhanced through bundles of free and pricey tickets to Washington-area sporting events that he supplied regularly to members and influential Hill staffers. Four Indian casino clients—the Choctaws, the Coushattas, the Chitimachas, and the Agua Caliente—at different times each paid between $200,000 and $300,000 annually to subsidize Abramoff's sky-boxes at three stadiums in the greater Washington area. Located at FedEx Field (football), the Verizon Center (basketball and ice hockey), and Camden Yards (baseball) in Baltimore, these sky-boxes together cost almost $1 million a year. "Abramoff really milked the skyboxes," recalled a former associate of the lobbyist who attended several events with him. "He always had someone of influence with him or a potential client."

Additionally, Abramoff's legendary fund-raising prowess, which depended heavily on his Indian casino clients, made his name synonymous with campaign loot for many Republican party committees and GOP leaders. "He's at the very top level of political fund-raising in the U.S.," one well-known GOP lobbyist and fund-raiser told me shortly after the scandal broke.

When Rudy and Volz separately pleaded guilty in 2006 to accepting bribes, they both acknowledged that, among other things, they had received free sporting tickets, meals, travel, and other financial benefits in exchange for legislative favors they did for Abramoff clients. Moreover, after Rudy and Volz left Capitol Hill and went into lobbying in 2001 and 2002, respectively, their pleas indicated that they conspired with Abramoff and Scanlon to provide similar favors to other public officials including Ney in exchange for legislative help. As the federal probe into Abramoff's influence peddling accelerated, the lobbyist's extensive entertaining of members and congressional staffers at Signatures and the skyboxes caught the eye of federal investigators and became a key focus.

Signatures became central to Abramoff's influence-peddling operation. Dozens of GOP members used Signatures to host fund-raisers in 2002 and 2003, ranging from Dennis Hastert to John Doolittle to David Vitter, a Republican from Louisiana. But on several occasions, members failed to report fully the costs of the event as they were required to do in their filings with the Federal Election Commission, and also failed to reimburse Signatures for their in-kind expenses. In early 2005, when ethical and legal concerns escalated over Abramoff's influence peddling, Hastert and Vitter belatedly repaid the restaurant for the cost of hosting their fund-raisers.

Ney, according to records, paid Signatures $1,900 for food and events between 2002 and 2004, but sources have said that he also ate there numerous times for free. In June 2002, Ney also attended a small dinner there with Abramoff, Volz, and a few representatives from one of the firm's more unusual clients—the General Council of Islamic Banks. The Bahrain-based group had sent representatives to Washington in an attempt to assure U.S. regulators that the group's banks were not connected in any way to terrorist financing. But the group was controversial and caused some embarrassment for Abramoff because of the background of its chairman, Saudi businessman Saleh Abdullah Kamel. In the 1980s, Kamel had been a major investor in a Sudanese bank that was used heavily by Osama bin Laden. Brian Walsh, a spokesman for Ney, told me that it "should surprise no one" that Ney, who was active on Middle East issues and served on the House Financial Services Committee, met with Islamic banking officials.

The restaurant's reported comp list also became a political headache for some members as fallout from the Abramoff scandal spread. The comp list, which *The New York Times* described, had a special designation for "FOO Comp," or friends of owner. Eighteen current and former members, lobbyists, and lawyers reportedly made the exclusive list. Laura Clifton, who once managed the dining room at Signatures, told the *Times* that guests frequently dined with Abramoff and never received checks. "They would come in for lunch with Jack and they wouldn't get a bill," Clifton said. Signatures, she added, was a "showplace and it was for business. It was all business all the time." Overall, records show that during a period in 2002 and 2003, $180,000 in free meals and drinks were given away.

Congressional ethics rules permit members to accept gifts from personal friends, but members are limited to gifts of under $100 a year from a single person and any individual gift must be valued under $50. Some members who were identified as getting free meals don't deny it and point to the friendship exemption in defense. "Just because you are a member of Congress doesn't mean you have to give up your friendships," Rohrabacher told the *Times*, noting that he had known Abramoff for two decades. Rohrabacher also said that he tried to take Abramoff out regularly and treated him to meals in return. DeLay and Ney, who were said to be on the comp list, have indicated they fully complied with gift regulations. A spokesman for Abramoff told the *Times* that "there has never been a comp list at Signatures authorized by Mr. Abramoff."

To be sure, Abramoff's varied use of Signatures for entertainment and business purposes was an expensive proposition. According to records, the lobbyist poured many millions of his casino profits into the venture. In just one period from January 2002 to May 2003, records show that Abramoff and his companies funneled some $3 million into Signatures.

Abramoff also tapped his tribal clients for extra funds to keep Signatures humming. Sometimes the tribes helped in ways they never even knew about. In at least one case, a $500,000 donation that the Mississippi Choctaws made to Abramoff's Capital Athletic Foundation proved very helpful in getting Signatures up and running. Right after the check arrived at the foundation in early January 2002, a $200,000 transfer from the foundation was made to Livsar, Abramoff's corporate entity that owned Signatures. The money was transferred back a few weeks later, but it came in handy. An Abramoff colleague wrote a grateful e-mail right after the funds arrived, noting that a banker "really saved us today" by moving the funds quickly from the foundation to the restaurant in the weeks just before Signatures opened.

Four lobbyists, two of whom worked with Abramoff at Greenberg Traurig, also point out that the tribes often received expense bills from Greenberg Traurig that included hefty tabs for meals at Signatures that sometimes left them puzzled and upset. A few tribes, according to sources, received expense bills that averaged $8,000 to $12,000 a month. In a few cases, these bills were on top of the tribes' monthly retainers that ranged as high as $180,000 with Abramoff and Greenberg Traurig.

Several tribal lobbyists have indicated that Abramoff may have improperly billed tribes for some expenses. One striking example was a humongous lunch bill for $4,000 at Signatures in December 2002 that was submitted to the Agua Caliente. And the tribe was sent a bill the next month that included a charge of $2,500 for a Super Bowl party at Stacks, another Abramoff-run eatery and Jewish delicatessen. Overall, during the nineteen months that the tribe retained Abramoff and his firm, the tribe's monthly expenses averaged about $12,000, a figure that some lawyers familiar with the probe think may have been padded. "There were clearly expenses that were inappropriate that were being passed along to the tribe [even though] they were not directly related to work on behalf of the client," said a source familiar with the investigation. But, he added, these expenses "were related to the interests of Jack Abramoff and others at his firm."

Looking back at the Signatures enterprise, which closed finally in late 2005, some former colleagues of the lobbyist remain awed by how much money went into it and the lavishness of its operations. "There was entertaining on a scale that I'd never seen before," Ron Platt, a Democratic lobbyist and former associate of Abramoff's at Greenberg Traurig, told me. "It was entertaining on a higher level. All I know is that people [lobbyists] were encouraged to spend every evening at Signatures wining and dining people. It was so blatantly a part of his lobbying practice."

Well before Signatures opened, Abramoff had perfected the art of mixing entertaining and fund-raising on a grand scale. By hitting up his Indian casino and other big clients yearly to the

tune of about $1 million, Abramoff used his four sports skyboxes
to woo new clients and Hill staffers, and raise campaign contributions for members, all of which redounded to his benefit. Typically, the skyboxes like the one at the Verizon Center had
Abramoff's name emblazoned on the doors and inside had pic-
tures, artwork, or memorabilia from different tribes like the
Choctaws and the Chitimachas. For instance, a *People* magazine
article about the Choctaws and Chief Martin was prominently
displayed at the Verizon Center box.

To help run his skybox enterprise, Abramoff set up Sports
Suites LLC, a separate company that one of his assistants
helped to coordinate at Preston Gates and later at Greenberg
Traurig. Funding came not only from four tribal clients but also
from two other megaclients, which had each given hundreds of
thousands to the U.S. Family Network. Both Willie Tan, the
Marianas garment tycoon who ran the eponymous Tan Holdings, and Alexander Koulakovsky of Naftasib at different times
funded the skyboxes. Even the U.S. Family Network kicked in
$149,000 one year to subsidize the Verizon Center boxes. The
group's former president, Pastor Chris Geeslin, told me that he
was kept in the dark about the check and learned of it only
somewhat by accident. One day, Geeslin said, he went to an
Orioles game and, after being introduced for the first time to
Abramoff, was taken aback to have him offer thanks for helping
finance the Verizon box.

The skyboxes served a few different roles in building
Abramoff's lobbying machine. For openers, the skyboxes were
useful in wooing congressional staffers who could be helpful
on legislative issues. To get the biggest return for his tickets,
Abramoff often used Tony Rudy, when he was DeLay's deputy
chief of staff, as a point man to give away free tickets to important staffers whom Abramoff was courting for help. Rudy earned
a reputation with other Hill aides as the "ticket dispenser" in

DeLay's office. "Several times a week there was an envelope on Tony's desk with scores of tickets from Abramoff," one ex–leadership aide told me. "Tony would use them to ply key staffers on issues. It was Tony's Ticketron."

Abramoff's skyboxes were used often to host relaxed meetings with potential clients. In late 2001, for instance, in one of Abramoff's classic moves to woo a new foreign client, he invited Khidir Haroun Ahmed, Sudan's ambassador to the United States, to join him at a Redskins game at FedEx Field. In between the action on the field, Abramoff unveiled a lobbying game plan with a multimillion-dollar price tag—according to one source as high as $18 million—to help the beleaguered government in Khartoum squelch criticism from conservative Christians in the United States. At the time, Sudan was under intense fire from American evangelical and human rights groups because of its widely reported persecution of Christians in the south. Khartoum also faced tough economic sanctions from Washington because of its links to terrorist groups.

Abramoff told Ahmed, according to a colleague familiar with his plan, that he could capitalize on his contacts with social conservatives to quash these critical voices and improve Sudan's image in the United States. In his pitch to the ambassador, Abramoff suggested that he would be able to enlist Ralph Reed to use his influence with evangelical groups such as the Christian Coalition to counter other religious critics and get Christian groups to change their positions. Abramoff suggested too that he would organize delegations to pay visits to Sudan. Andrew Blum, a spokesman for Abramoff, has said that the lobbyist never mentioned specific amounts of money and claimed that Abramoff strongly criticized Khartoum's policies.

But that's not the impression that Ahmed or Abramoff's former associate expressed to me in interviews in 2004. Ahmed told me that he didn't take Abramoff's proposal too seriously because it would have violated American laws. "I don't want to get people in trouble with the American legal system," Ahmed explained. Abramoff, according to his onetime associate, even suggested that if Sudan set up a foundation in England or Switzerland, there might be a way to circumvent the American economic sanctions. No deal was ever consummated with Sudan, though, because the government wanted some guarantees from the lobbyist that he could successfully change the positions of religious groups and Washington's official policies.

Besides courting clients at Oriole or Redskin games, Abramoff let members use the skyboxes to hold fund-raisers, as *The Washington Post* documented. Some six dozen fund-raising events were scheduled by Abramoff and his fellow lobbyists for the skyboxes from 1999 through 2003. Many of the money bashes were slated to be held for the lobbyist's major allies, including GOP members like DeLay, Doolittle, and J. D. Hayworth of Arizona. DeLay, for instance, used a skybox at the Verizon Center in May of 2000 to reward some of his big donors with tickets to a Three Tenors concert.

Doolittle was slated to use the skyboxes five different times, but a spokesman for the congressman said that he actually used it only once, in 1999. In that case, however, Doolittle apparently did not adhere to campaign finance rules that require that tickets be limited to $49 per person and be publicly reported. The skybox that Doolittle used had twenty seats and the tickets were valued at just under $50 a seat, which meant that the cost for the box was just under $1,000. Doolittle failed in his reporting to the Federal Election Commission to note the event as an in-kind contribution or to pay for the box, one of which was required. After the *Post* reported on this mistake, a Doolittle spokesperson said it would be corrected.

What's more, Abramoff found several other ways to flex his fund-raising muscle and burnish his image as a premier GOP fund-raiser. Not long after the scandal broke, another top GOP fund-raiser on K Street heaped praise on Abramoff: "He's worked hard to raise money for various political committees and campaigns." The fellow lobbyist added that Abramoff also might be "number one for congressional Republicans in terms of raising Jewish money." One of Abramoff's big triumphs in 2003 and early 2004 was to reach the magic mark of roping in $100,000 in donations for the Bush reelection campaign, earning him elite Pioneer status. As Bush fund-raising got rolling early in 2003, Abramoff was one of a few dozen Washington lobbyists who were invited to Crawford for a campaign rally one summer weekend at a ranch adjoining the president's. Because the outing would have required traveling on the Jewish Sabbath, Abramoff told me in 2003 he didn't attend.

At the time, well before Abramoff's name had become anathema in fund-raising circles, the lobbyist sounded quite bullish about how much money he would snag for Bush. Abramoff calmly informed me that before he finished his work for Bush, he expected to bring in $200,000 for the campaign and earn the even more elite Ranger title that the campaign bestowed on its biggest money men and women. "The difficulty that some lobbyists are having is that they don't have networks outside the Beltway," he quietly boasted to me. "As a consequence, they find that many of the people they're soliciting are also raising money or have already contributed themselves."

During Bush's reelection drive, the campaign put together a little-noticed effort in 2003 to mobilize top Jewish fund-raisers nationwide and target the Jewish community for more contributions and votes. Fred Zeidman, a Texas-based fund-raiser for the president and a friend of Abramoff's who later joined Greenberg Traurig as a lobbyist, was one of the prime movers in that effort, which also was aimed at boosting Bush's overall vote count in the Jewish community. Abramoff, who was trying to lend a hand too, told me in 2003 that he thought the Bush campaign's focus on the Jewish community for more votes and money was a smart one that "could be the difference" in some key states, such as Ohio, Florida, and Pennsylvania, with relatively large Jewish populations. Bush won the first two states but lost the latter. The lobbyist pointed out in 2003 that Bush's very strong backing for Israel—which many analysts have described as uncritical—would both help with Jewish voters and appeal to another key bloc: "I think evangelical supporters of the president are delighted by his strong support of Israel," Abramoff told me. On another front, *Newsweek* reported that during the Bush reelection drive, Rabbi Daniel Lapin prodded "friends and colleagues to steer campaign checks to Bush via Abramoff."

To be sure, Abramoff and his wife, Pam, were also big donors, and not surprisingly, their money went exclusively to Republicans. During the 2004 campaign, the lobbyist and his wife gave $83,000 to Republicans, a total that placed them ninety-third in the country in terms of donations to either party. Abramoff was especially generous to DeLay. From 1997 through early 2004, the lobbyist and his wife donated a total of $40,000 to DeLay's campaign and his leadership PAC, Americans for a Republican Majority.

But it was via the very deep pockets of his clients that Abramoff exerted exceptional influence on Capitol Hill. A study in late 2005 by the nonpartisan Center for Responsive Politics dramatized the breadth of his fund-raising. The survey found that since 1999, 210 members of Congress had received donations from Abramoff, his Indian casino clients, and SunCruz. The study calculated that the top twenty-five recipients of Abramoff-related donations raked in $21,500 or more. Of this elite group, only five were Democrats and twenty were Republicans, with Senator Conrad Burns leading the pack.

Typically, Abramoff's tribal clients received detailed lists of his recommendations for campaign contributions once or twice a year. The lists usually featured dozens of suggested donations for members, party committees, and even conservative allies such as Norquist's ATR, sometimes mixing the three areas together. Quite often, tribal lobbyists told me, Abramoff dropped DeLay's name as an incentive to get them to write checks. "DeLay's name was the punch line to convince the council that we either needed to make donations or to keep employing Abramoff and Scanlon," Bernie Sprague of the Saginaw Chippewas recalled.

It regularly proved an effective strategy. In early 2002, the Chippewas donated $18,000 to DeLay's ARMPAC and wrote a check for $15,000 more to the Republican National Committee. The Chippewas also heard DeLay's name in another fundraising gambit. In a 2002 memo sent to the Chippewas that was released by the Indian Affairs Committee, the tribe was hit up simultaneously for three $25,000 checks to Norquist's ATR, the National Republican Congressional Committee, and Abramoff's Capital Athletic Foundation. The memo stated that DeLay "assists in raising money" for the foundation. Other tribes also often heard DeLay's name invoked by Abramoff, according to e-mails and documents released by the Indian Affairs Committee.

Abramoff often demonstrated a keen sense of timing by tapping his clients for money at almost the precise moment they were seeking help from particular members. One clear example of this tactic occurred during the battles between the Coushattas and the Jenas in 2002, when contributions came pouring in to several Democratic and Republican members in close proximity to letters they wrote backing his casino client. For example, after Senate minority leader Harry Reid of Nevada was lobbied by his onetime Hill aide Eddie Ayoob, who was an Abramoff-lobbying colleague, the Democratic leader cosigned a March 5,

2002, letter with GOP Senator John Ensign of Nevada that opposed the Jenas' casino effort. The very next day, the Coushattas sent a $5,000 check to Reid's leadership PAC and a little later Reid received another $5,000 check from a different tribal casino client of Abramoff's.

Similarly, in late February 2002, when twenty-seven lawmakers signed a letter to Gale Norton opposing the Jenas, more than two-thirds of them received contributions from Abramoff or his clients, or used Signatures for fund-raisers, according to an Associated Press report. As usual, the lion's share of the tribal largesse went to GOP members. For instance, Doolittle received a $1,000 donation from Abramoff shortly before he signed the joint letter to Norton and also got checks for $16,000 a couple of months later from two tribal clients of Abramoff's. For his part, Representative Pete Sessions, a Texas Republican who also signed the letter, received $5,500 in tribal donations about a month later.

Abramoff's tribal largesse was also apparently used in some unorthodox ways by Scanlon, according to former colleagues of the two influence merchants. In late October 2002, Capitol Campaign Strategies made two contributions of $250,000 each to the Republican Governors Association, a group that works to boost the party's share of gubernatorial seats. The Scanlon company contributions, which were the largest that the RGA received during that election season, came in unsolicited and were not earmarked for any particular race, RGA spokesman Harvey Valentine told me in 2004. But sources familiar with the donations have said that they were part of an effort by Abramoff and the Choctaws to influence a hotly contested race between then representative Bob Riley, a GOP member and a foe of gambling, and then Alabama governor Don Siegelman, a Democrat, who was in favor of legalizing some gambling in the state. Riley, whom Scanlon had briefly worked for before he joined DeLay, won the race by a very slim margin of 3,120 votes out of some 1.3 million that were cast.

On October 17, 2002, the very same day that the RGA deposited the first check for $250,000 from Scanlon, it sent $350,000 to Riley's campaign and another $150,000 to the state GOP in Alabama. A second check from Scanlon for $250,000 arrived a few days later at the RGA's headquarters. Valentine said that the timing of the transfer and the Scanlon checks was simply coincidence and that the RGA was "raising money all across the country and spending it across the country." But a top GOP fund-raiser told me he thought that the RGA's explanations of the Scanlon donations were implausible. "Contributions of that size don't come in unsolicited," he caustically commented. The Choctaws declined to comment, but former Abramoff colleagues told me that the funds originated with the tribe, which was consistent with their longtime posture of fighting off gaming threats in neighboring Alabama.

The influence machine built by Abramoff extended well beyond fund-raising and entertaining for GOP politicians and staffers. Abramoff was equally legendary for handing out all sorts of perks, like overseas junkets and monetary remuneration for numerous conservative allies, including writers and opinion makers. Rabbi Daniel Lapin, in defending Abramoff not long after the scandal broke in 2004, told me that allegations of misconduct amount to a "politically driven witch hunt against the extremely effective conservative matrix of alliances constructed and nurtured by Jack."

In a slightly more oblique but equally grandiose tribute to Abramoff in 2004, Ralph Reed informed me that Abramoff was a "different kind of lobbyist." Reed likened Abramoff to then star GOP lobbyists Ed Gillespie and Haley Barbour, both of whom at different times served as chairman of the Republican National Committee. Abramoff, Reed told me, is "more identified as a strategist and builder of the Republican majority than for his lobbying practice alone. His business is largely a means to that end."

In a sense, Reed and Lapin were making similar points and using somewhat euphemistic language. They both were suggesting—without explicitly saying so—that Abramoff used his lobbying talents and his clients' largesse to support GOP political projects and causes that the lobbyist and his friends alike viewed as instrumental in creating a stronger conservative base.

To be sure, Abramoff the strategist often blended in smoothly with Abramoff the canny and cynical lobbyist who pushed his clients' images and interests by sharing their funds with fellow conservatives. Some of his lobbying booty—particularly from the Choctaws and the Marianas—flowed into the hands of conservative writers who penned articles favorable to Abramoff clients. In perhaps the most blatant example of a conservative writer for hire, *BusinessWeek* reported in 2005 that Doug Bandow, a long-time senior fellow at the Cato Institute and a syndicated columnist for Copley News Service, had over several years accepted thousands of dollars from Abramoff to write between one and two dozen articles. According to an e-mail released by McCain's committee, Bandow received $10,000 in 1996, which was funneled from Abramoff's clients through Ridenour's National Center for Public Policy Research. Bandow owned up to a "lapse in judgment" and Cato sacked him in late 2005 soon after the story ran. Over the years, Bandow wrote glowing pieces—some for payments of $2,000—about the Marianas and also about the Choctaws, hailing the latter for their entrepreneurial spirit. "The Choctaws offer a model for other tribes," Bandow once wrote in his syndicated column.

Another scribe whom Abramoff put to good use was Peter Ferrara, a conservative policy analyst who was long affiliated with Norquist's Americans for Tax Reform and then moved to

the Institute for Policy Innovation. Ferrara too has acknowledged, though seemingly with some pride, that he took thousands of dollars from the lobbyist to tout Abramoff's clients.
Ferrara confided to *BusinessWeek* in 2005 that "I do that all the
time. I've done that in the past and I'll do in the future." Ferrara
argued that there was nothing wrong with the practice, since in
his case all the views that he espoused in his columns were in
accord with his ideological principles. Some of Ferrara's favorable pieces on the Choctaws and the Marianas wound up in *The
Washington Times*, a conservative paper owned by South Korea's
Reverend Sun Myung Moon, the leader of the cultish Unifica-
tion Church.

Early in his K Street career, Abramoff launched an even
broader ideological and lobbying drive on behalf of the Marianas
with help from his conservative friends. Abramoff's plan was to
enlist a who's who of Washington conservatives to go to bat for
the Marianas' cause, an effort that boiled down to protecting
their cherished exemptions from U.S. minimum wage and labor
laws. At Abramoff's urging, the Marianas shelled out hundreds
of thousands of dollars in the mid- to late 1990s to send conservative heavyweights from the Heritage Foundation, the Traditional Values Coalition, the Cato Institute, Citizens Against
Government Waste, and Citizens for a Sound Economy on all-
expense-paid trips to the islands. Other conservatives from
Norquist's ATR and Citizens Against Government Waste went to
the Marianas and returned to initiate aggressive lobbying campaigns to protect the islands' garment makers from losing one of
their special privileges, the right to place "Made in the USA" la-
bels on their exports.

The conservative blitz in Washington was crucial to counter-
ing the growing threats that the islands' exemptions faced
in Congress, even from some key Republicans like former senator Frank Murkowski of Alaska. In 2000, Murkowski chaired the

Senate Energy and Natural Resources Committee. The senator was outraged by testimony indicating that the islands' heavily immigrant workforce was subjected to brutal working conditions, and he wrote a bill to give the Marianas the protection of U.S. labor laws and the U.S. minimum wage. The bill unanimously passed the Senate, as some similar measures had done before, but was blocked in the House by DeLay's efforts. Abramoff, whose billing records indicate that he met personally with the congressman about two dozen times over a two-year period and many more times with DeLay's staffers, can take much of the credit for the defeat of such measures.

George Miller of California, who for years was the chief Democrat in the House pushing labor reform bills for the Marianas, has bitter memories of lobbying fights with DeLay and Abramoff. "DeLay's office was there to obstruct any effort to reform that abusive system," Miller told me in an interview shortly before DeLay announced he was retiring from Congress. "What's very clear now is that Abramoff had the full run of DeLay's office for that purpose."

SEVEN

Conduits Are Us

■

When it was launched in early 2001, the American International Center's Web site described its mission in grandiose terms: "AIC is determined to influence global paradigms in an increasingly complex world. Based in sunny Rehoboth Beach, Delaware, the AIC staff is using 21st century technology and decades of experience to make the world a smaller place. In summary the AIC is bringing great minds together from all over the globe." The Web site also referred proudly to the "high powered directorship" of AIC by David Grosh and Brian Mann. It turned out that Grosh and Mann were both old pals of Scanlon from Rehoboth Beach who worked, respectively, as a lifeguard and a yoga instructor. After he left DeLay's office, despite his multimillion-dollar beach home, Scanlon himself worked part-time as a lifeguard.

The think tank itself was housed in a very modest yellow beach bungalow that I visited briefly one rainy summer day in 2005. It was located at 53 Baltimore Avenue, on a street filled with several chic and expensive boutiques, arts and crafts shops, and restaurants. The key mission of the think tank was basically to serve as a pass-through-conduit for almost $2.3 million in tribal funds that were channeled to Ralph Reed to pay for work he did for the Coushattas, and to help disguise about $1.5 million in payments that the Malaysian government was sending to Abramoff and his firm for lobbying work.

The Rehoboth Beach think tank was just one of several conduits and shells that Abramoff used to disguise and divert millions of dollars in funds supplied by his Indian casino clients as well as some corporate and foreign clients. Using these pipelines, the lobbyist effectively hid enormous sums of money from public scrutiny and directed the cash into his own pet projects and pockets, as well as those of his friends and political cronies.

Besides AIC, Abramoff channeled some $6 million from tribal and other clients through the Capital Athletic Foundation—his own personal charity that was instrumental in funding the Eshkol Academy.

For other assistance in moving money covertly, Abramoff used a few old conservative friends who ran think tanks or other nonprofit organizations that he helped to bankroll. At times, Abramoff turned to groups run by his oldest political comrades, such as Grover Norquist's Americans for Tax Reform and Amy Ridenour's National Center for Public Policy Research, to funnel casino funds and other client monies that Abramoff wanted to keep hidden. He also used even more obscure entities, such as Toward Tradition, Rabbi Daniel Lapin's conservative Jewish group of which he was a longtime board member.

Although AIC was set up as a corporation, most of the other groups that Abramoff used as conduits were tax-exempt organizations and charities. In a press conference shortly after Abramoff's plea, Mark Everson, the commissioner of the Internal Revenue Service, underscored the seriousness of the abuses committed by the lobbyist. "One of the most disturbing elements of his whole sordid story is the blatant misuse of charities in a scheme to peddle political influence."

These kinds of entities are typically given special tax status by the IRS because they ostensibly serve a public purpose, but the lobbyist exploited these vehicles for mostly mercenary reasons. Abramoff's influence-peddling schemes with charities and other groups that he used as shells involved financial transactions that could be dizzyingly complex: millions of dollars sometimes went into foundations or think tanks and then were transferred not once, but sometimes twice, before reaching their final destination.

AIC, the Rehoboth Beach–based think tank that Scanlon set up in 2001 shortly after Abramoff had joined Greenberg Traurig, was located just a five-minute walk from the shoreline where the former DeLay aide had spent summers as a teenager.

With regard to Malaysia, the think tank acted basically as a conduit to send funds from Kuala Lumpur to Abramoff's firm Greenberg Traurig. By funneling $1.2 million through AIC, which never disclosed its ties to the Malaysian government, both the think tank and Greenberg Traurig skirted the legal requirement that foreign agents register with a Justice Department's Foreign Agents Registration Unit. Instead, the lobbying firm filed a lobbying registration with Congress to ostensibly represent the American International Center on economic matters. For that work, which began in mid-2001, AIC paid Greenberg Traurig $1.5 million.

At the time, Malaysia had a serious image problem in the United States. Malaysian prime minister Mahathir Mohamad had a history of making anti-Semitic comments, had a poor human rights record, and had jailed one key political critic, Finance Minister Anwar Ibrahim, on trumped-up charges of sodomy. Abramoff's mission for Malaysia was twofold: get members of Congress to visit Malaysia and also try to arrange for a much-coveted meeting at the White House with President Bush. In terms of getting members to visit Kuala Lumpur,

Abramoff and his team had very limited success. In January of 2002, Tony Rudy and another colleague at Greenberg Traurig escorted a handful of members on a trip to Malaysia, including Republicans Dana Rohrabacher and Pete Sessions and Democrat Gregory Meeks.

Arranging for a meeting in Washington or in Asia between Mahathir and Bush initially proved difficult—especially given Mahathir's track record. On September 10, 2001, Abramoff reached out to Ralph Reed for help with the White House. President Bush and Mahathir were both slated to attend an economic summit in October hosted by the Asian Pacific Economic Cooperation (APEC) forum, and Abramoff wanted Reed to prod Rove to help arrange a meeting between the two leaders at the summit. In his e-mail to Reed, Abramoff wrote, "I have a one month subcontract for you if you can help me. We need to get to Rove to see if we can break through the current posture of State on Malaysia and the PM meeting with Bush at the APEC meeting at the beginning of October . . . If it works, there will be a lot more." Reed wrote back, "Sure." It's not clear whether Reed actually did any work on Malaysia.

But after September 11, the situation improved in part because Malaysia became an early ally in the "war against terrorism." Bush and Mahathir did meet briefly at the APEC summit in October. A former associate of Abramoff's who was familiar with the Malaysia work told me that the lobbyist boasted that he talked to Karl Rove at least once to push for a Washington meeting between Bush and Mahathir. The associate said that he was with Abramoff one day when he received a call from someone in the White House indicating that an invitation for Mahathir to meet with Bush "was on its way." An official meeting between the Malaysian leader and Bush took place in the White House on May 14, 2002, and later that day the Malaysian prime minister was the featured guest at a dinner at the Malaysian embassy in Washington that Abramoff attended. During the course of the Malaysia work, Greenberg Traurig apparently became apprehensive about how Abramoff and Scanlon were using AIC to circumvent the Foreign Agents Registration Act. The firm asked Trevor Potter, a well-known Republican election law and ethics expert and a former chairman of the Federal Election Commission, for his legal opinion on whether the firm needed to register for its Malaysia work. Potter wrote a detailed memo that raised strong concerns about how AIC was being used to disguise the Malaysia work that the firm was doing, and questioned its legality. Potter's memo further questioned whether AIC was truly a legitimate and independent entity given that it was headed by Scanlon, who had been working for Abramoff.

When Potter's memo came into Greenberg Traurig, Abramoff went ballistic, according to former colleagues. Potter's memo prompted the firm to ask AIC several questions including whether the funds came from the Malaysian government. An infuriated Abramoff quickly huddled with Scanlon, who in turn provided the law firm with sketchy answers, according to sources familiar with the Malaysia work.

In mid-January 2002, Abramoff started sending e-mails to Tony Rudy and other colleagues that attacked Potter's position on the think tank and referred to him as "pothead." Abramoff decided to retaliate against Potter and, with Rudy's help, succeeded in getting DeLay to put a brief statement in the *Congressional Record* that disparaged Potter, a leading advocate of campaign finance reform, for some of his views on limiting campaign contributions. On January 25, 2002, Rudy e-mailed DeLay's office suggesting language for a statement on Potter that was very similar to what DeLay put in the *Congressional Record* on February 13, 2002, according to a source familiar with the

Rudy e-mail. The DeLay statement, which was only three sentences long, contained two factual errors: it referred incorrectly to Potter as a lobbyist for the Campaign Finance Institute and as a board member of Common Cause.

AIC performed a slightly different kind of washing operation with Indian casino funds. Two of Abramoff's tribal clients, the Coushattas and the Choctaws, were directed to send almost $6 million to the think tank, which then sent along AIC checks to Reed's Century Strategies, in much the same fashion that Norquist's antitax group had previously done. Sources familiar with the scheme say that Norquist had tired of serving as a conduit and had grown skittish about the arrangement. E-mails indicate that Abramoff and Scanlon had to locate a new entity to satisfy Reed's desire for secrecy. From March through May 2001, according to records released by the Senate Indian Affairs Committee, the think tank sent about $2.3 million to Century Strategies and an affiliate. There's no doubt that the two men placed a premium on stealth to hide Reed's funds. Once in 2001, when Reed voiced dismay at late payments, Abramoff helpfully e-mailed his old friend: "The originating entity had to transfer to a separate account before they transferred it to the entity which is going to transfer it to you."

At different times during the Senate probe, Reed's explanation about his antigambling work shifted. In 2004 when I interviewed him, he told me that he never worked for a casino or was paid by one; later he stressed that Abramoff assured him that no funds sent to him came from gambling enterprises. But e-mails continued to be released by the Senate committee that showed Reed should have known that the Coushattas, which had only gambling revenues, were the source of about half the $6 million he was paid. Ultimately, Reed's ties to Abramoff and his lucrative Indian casino lobbying became a big political headache during his campaign in 2006 to become Georgia's lieutenant

governor. In early 2006 on the campaign trail, a somewhat beleaguered Reed was quoted in the Georgia papers as saying, "If I
had known then what I know now, I would not have done that
work."

Overall for Reed's work on antigambling projects in Louisiana, Texas, and Alabama, Reed's Century Strategies received
payments not only from AIC and ATR but also from Capitol
Campaign Strategies and Preston Gates. The fees paid to Reed's
firm totaled almost $6 million, according to documents and
sources.

Scanlon's AIC received plenty of attention—some of it quite
zany and amusing—when one of the Indian Affairs Committee
hearings in mid-2005 called Grosh and Mann to testify. While
Mann "took the Fifth" and appeared stolid, Grosh surprised and
entertained the audience with some refreshingly candid statements about his work with Scanlon, whom he'd known since
they were teenagers.

Grosh, whose slightly rumpled appearance and deadpan de-
livery made him sound a bit like a latter-day Jefferson Smith
(*Mr. Smith Goes to Washington*), told the panel that Scanlon had
called him one day with an intriguing offer. Scanlon asked, "Do
you want to be head of an international corporation?" Grosh allowed that the invitation was "a hard one to turn down." When
Grosh inquired of Scanlon what the job entailed, Scanlon made
the offer even sweeter, answering, "Nothing." "So that sounded
pretty good to me," Grosh conceded.

With a twinkle in his eye, Senator McCain asked Grosh if he
had attended any meetings. Grosh said he went to one, and Mc-
Cain zeroed in, asking how long it lasted. "Fifteen minutes,"
Grosh answered, adding that he couldn't recall any details about
what was discussed. Nonetheless, Grosh said he was paid a total
of $2,500 for his labors and got some free tickets to a hockey
game. But Grosh hastened to add that when it started to smell

like a risky deal, he resigned. "I got out of it when I found out it involved the federal government, Indian tribes and gambling." Looking back at the experience with Scanlon, Grosh added that he was "embarrassed and disgusted to be part of this whole thing."

AIC's missions were quite different from Abramoff's Capital Athletic Foundation, but both organizations shared the lobbyist's penchant for using covert funding mechanisms. When Abramoff set up the foundation in 1999, it was touted as a kind of all-American effort to promote good sportsmanship and help the less privileged.

The group's Web site prominently featured small grants—most of them less than $10,000—to a variety of well-known organizations ranging from a local Boy Scout troop to the YMCA of Metropolitan Washington. The foundation's Web site also trumpeted its backing of "needy and deserving" programs to foster sportsmanship.

So it came as a rude shock to some of the biggest donors to learn where the bulk of the monies really were spent. During its four years of existence, only a tiny fraction of the $6 million it raised actually went directly to sports programs. Far and away the largest beneficiary of the foundation was the Eshkol Academy, the short-lived Jewish prep school in suburban Maryland that Abramoff had founded and that was attended by two of his sons. According to the foundation's records, about 70 percent of the $6 million went to the academy. In 2002 alone, Eshkol received a grant of $1.8 million, while all the other recipients that year were given just $500,000.

Overall, at least four of Abramoff's tribal clients helped bankroll the foundation. The Coushattas and the Choctaws gave $1 million apiece in 2001 and 2002, respectively, although the Coushattas were tricked into making their donation and never informed that their $1 million payment was actually going to the foundation. Hundreds of thousands more came from a few other Abramoff clients and Amy Ridenour's National Center for Public Policy Research, on whose board Abramoff served.

For extra fund-raising help for CAF, Abramoff even turned to Julie Doolittle, the wife of Representative John Doolittle. From mid-2002 until February 2004, a small Virginia-based company called Sierra Dominion Financial Services that the congressman's wife ran was paid about $5,000 a month by Greenberg Traurig, netting Julie Doolittle about $96,000. The funds came out of the monthly fees that the Agua Caliente tribe was paying to the firm, according to sources familiar with the arrangement. During this time, Julie Doolittle was helping to organize a gala fund-raiser for the foundation at Washington's International Spy Museum, which was cancelled because of the start of the Iraq war. Early in the Justice probe of Abramoff's lobbying, Julie Doolittle's company received a subpoena from the grand jury requesting information about its dealings with Abramoff. A spokeswoman for the congressman, Laura Blackann, has said there was no connection between Julie Doolittle's work for Abramoff and the congressman.

In one fund-raising gambit in 2001, Abramoff never asked the Coushattas to give a $1 million donation directly to his nonprofit. Instead, Abramoff pulled off what was essentially a double scam involving both the tribe and Greenberg Traurig. According to testimony and records from a Senate hearing in the fall of 2005, the Coushattas were tricked into making the donation with some help from Scanlon. Abramoff told his associate that he wanted to route the funds first through his lobbying firm to boost its standing in the lobbying rankings, always a key preoccupation for the lobbyist. Scanlon agreed to cooperate and sent the Coushattas a phony invoice on the firm's letterhead for $1 million for unspecified "public affairs services."

Even though Scanlon misspelled one of the firm's name

lawyers by writing "Greenburg" on the fake bill, the tribe complied. Once the tribal payment came in to Greenberg Traurig, Abramoff misled his colleagues by telling them that the tribe wanted to donate the funds to his foundation. Greenberg Traurig, taking Abramoff's word, complied with his request. All the time, however, the tribe knew nothing about the foundation, and his firm was deceived as well.

The ruse might have been prompted in part to avoid scrutiny by Bert Langley, the Coushatta treasurer. Langley told me that if a request for a $1 million donation to CAF had come in from Abramoff, he "would have questioned it," since he had become suspicious of other large sums that the tribe was paying to the lobbyist and Scanlon. "I was concerned about too much money going out without proper documentation." Ultimately, when tribal leaders understood Abramoff's scam, they were dismayed. "In my personal view, this payment reveals the extent of Mr. Abramoff's shamelessness," Coushatta council member David Sickey told the Senate panel in 2005 at one of its hearings.

From the foundation's start, subsidizing the Eshkol Academy was clearly its major, though never public, mission. Eshkol, which existed for a little over two years, was launched by Abramoff in the fall of 2002 after he'd grown dissatisfied with another Jewish school in the Washington area where two of his sons had been students. During its brief existence, Eshkol attracted between sixty and one hundred students, who offered mixed reviews about its operations and success.

The school was always struggling to make ends meet, and the scramble for funds preoccupied Abramoff. To judge by some of his urgent e-mails on the subject to Scanlon, there were times when the foundation and Eshkol became almost interchangeable as he sought more money. In February 2003, for instance, Abramoff e-mailed Scanlon, "Please make sure the next $1 million from Coushatta for me goes to Eshkol Academy directly.

Please tell them that we are using the school as our conduit for some of our activities." Abramoff then quickly added that "if that won't fly with them use CAF." It's unclear whether Scanlon ever followed through on this effort.

The school ceased operations in mid-2004, not long after the scandal had forced Abramoff out of his law firm and his financial situation had become increasingly precarious. After it went out of business, thirteen teachers filed a suit for $140,000 in back pay that they claimed they were owed and some went public with criticisms of Abramoff's management of the educational venture. The lawsuit charged that the Capital Athletic Foundation was used "to launder" funds for the school.

One of the plaintiffs in the suit, Samuel Whitehill, who taught Hebrew at Eshkol, has been outspoken about the school's treatment of its former faculty. He likened the school to a "Greek tragedy" and charged that it was "totally unable to function as an educational institution." The former faculty member told me that a key administrator was Rabbi David Lapin (the brother of Rabbi Daniel Lapin), who ran a California-based consulting firm called Strategic Business Ethics. Yet Lapin, who was paid about $60,000 a year, was rarely at the school, Whitehill recalled.

Eshkol wasn't the only Abramoff project where the lobbyist asked David Lapin to lend a hand, work that was paid for—indirectly or directly—by Abramoff's clients. Lapin received a controversial no-bid contract from the Marianas in the mid-1990s for $1.2 million to do an "ethics in government" study for the islands' government. Pam Brown, the attorney general for the Marianas, raised questions in an interview with *The New York Times* in 2005 about what Lapin actually produced for the islands' government. Lapin defended his role to me, arguing that the "government was satisfied with my work," which he said included an employee handbook and a code of ethics.

Abramoff helped Lapin secure other consulting jobs. Lapin spent about half his time over a three-year period in the late 1990s working on a project for the Mississippi Choctaws that Abramoff helped steer his way, he said. Lapin produced a manual about how casinos could get to know their customers and employees better.

Lapin recalled that he first met Abramoff in South Africa during the filming of *Red Scorpion* in the late 1980s when the neophyte filmmaker was a dinner guest at his home. Paul Erickson, Abramoff's old friend from College Republicans who worked on the movie, told me that Lapin was a formative influence on Abramoff's Judaism. Other former lobbying colleagues of Abramoff's told me that Lapin had other talents that the lobbyist utilized—including handwriting analysis. During his years at Preston Gates, Abramoff on a few occasions sent Lapin handwriting samples of a few prospective assistants for his analysis, before he made his hiring decisions.

Lapin's Eshkol work wasn't the only instance where an old friend of Abramoff's benefited financially from Abramoff's foundation. One of the more bizarre athletic foundation projects was Abramoff's channeling of $140,000 to a sniper school in the West Bank town of Beitar Illit, where Shmuel Ben-Zvi, an old friend of Abramoff's from Los Angeles, had been living. The town's mayor, Yitzhak Pindrus, told *Newsweek* that Ben-Zvi was a well-known advocate for improving security and even spearheaded his own patrol operations.

Abramoff was a devoted and fierce backer of Israel, and apparently he couldn't resist an appeal for badly needed assistance from his old friend, according to e-mails and documents released by Senate investigators. Among the items purchased by Abramoff, according to foundation records, were sniper scopes, a thermal imager, night-vision binoculars, and some camouflage gear and other equipment that the foundation's records some-what euphemistically call "security" equipment.

A grateful Ben-Zvi on August 13, 2002, wrote Abramoff, thanking him effusively for the equipment he'd arranged for his friend—including the thermal imager, which may have been facilitated by Abramoff's Russian client Marina Nevskaya with the energy company Naftasib, according to e-mails. One intriguing e-mail to Abramoff came from an assistant to Nevskaya named Vadim, who provided prices for thermal vision equipment, a bit of information that he probably had access to since Nevskaya reportedly had ties to military security in Moscow. In his August note to Abramoff, Ben-Zvi wrote, "And now that I'll have wheels, I'll be much more effective. You did this for me brother. It really breathes new life into me." Abramoff plainly appreciated his friend's efforts. In an e-mail response Abramoff wrote, "Thanks Brother. If only there were another dozen of you the dirty rats would be finished."

But there were apparently some minor logistical and accounting headaches in forwarding the funds to Ben-Zvi in the West Bank. Gail Halpern, Abramoff's accountant, urged him to send the monies through a nonprofit or educational entity in Israel to avoid IRS hassles, and ultimately most of the funds were channeled to a school called Kollel Tikrit, which served as a cover for the payments to Ben-Zvi.

At one juncture, when Abramoff was brainstorming about how to discreetly arrange the covert payments to Ben-Zvi for his sniper operations, the lobbyist betrayed his own anxieties too. According to an e-mail to Abramoff from one of his assistants in September 2002, Ben-Zvi apparently had made a suggestion that caused Abramoff to blanch. The lobbyist's assistant, Allison Bozniak, told Abramoff that his friend could provide a letter to him with his "Sniper Workshop logo" on it. And trying her best to be helpful, she added that this is some sort of "educational entity."

Abramoff quickly rebuffed her. "No don't do that. I don't want a sniper letterhead."

It's easy to see why Abramoff would react so vociferously to having a sniper letterhead in any way linked to his foundation, especially since other funds were going for travel projects like the $150,000 that was used to pay for the lobbyist's and Bob Ney's Scotland junket in August 2002. The rush to raise funds for the foundation to cover the trip's cost was particularly intense. It involved not only Abramoff but also his colleague Tony Rudy, according to e-mails that the Senate committee released. Rudy, according to Abramoff's plea bargain, seemed to be working furiously to help Abramoff raise big bucks for the Ney excursion.

In addition to the $50,000 for the foundation that Abramoff secured with help from the Tiguas, Rudy solicited another lobbying client, the Russian company SPI Spirits, which in the post-Soviet period bought Stolichnaya. A $25,000 donation was made to the foundation by SPI within weeks of a lobbying drive that Rudy helped to spearhead on Capitol Hill. In that effort, Rudy turned to former boss Dana Rohrabacher of California for help. Rudy and the Greenberg team were lobbying for Hill support for SPI's position in a complex dispute that the company was having with the Russian government; in 2001 Moscow issued a controversial ruling that SPI's purchase was illegal, precipitating years of litigation. To help SPI, Rudy and his colleagues were trying to get the U.S. government to put some heat on Moscow. On May 21, 2002, in a letter to the U.S. trade representative, Rohrabacher backed SPI's position in its fight. The letter was signed by seventeen other members of Congress.

But at times Rudy and Abramoff ran into trouble with their

colleagues as they aggressively sought funds for the foundation. In one case, Rudy apparently misunderstood directions from Abramoff and mistakenly approached his associate Todd Boulanger for help on the fund-raising. But when Boulanger was first asked by Rudy to raise $25,000 from a tribe for the foundation, he was taken aback and reacted with suspicion. "What is this?" Boulanger e-mailed Rudy. "I've never heard of it." Rudy responded that "Jack wants this." But Boulanger wasn't buying it: "I'm sensing shadiness. I'll stop asking." At that point Rudy alerted Abramoff, who became enraged that Boulanger had been contacted at all and scolded Rudy for not following instructions.

Abramoff's flare-up over Rudy's fund-raising gaffe came on the heels of much more serious tensions that had been developing for some time between Rudy and Scanlon. Even though Scanlon was mostly working directly and secretly with Abramoff on Indian casino projects outside the firm, Rudy had gleaned—almost from his first days as a lobbyist in early 2001—that he wasn't making nearly as much money as Scanlon. The jealousies and rivalries between the two men over money matters were intense, according to a few of their former associates. Scanlon and Rudy often badmouthed each other to colleagues and even leaked negative tidbits to friendly reporters to undermine each other. By mid-2002, Rudy was fed up. When he received an offer from Ed Buckham, an old friend and former chief of staff to DeLay, to join the Alexander Strategy Group, he jumped ship.

Unlike Rudy, Amy Ridenour of the National Center for Public Policy Research didn't perceive Scanlon as a rival when Abramoff suggested sending funds his way for some projects. For almost seven years, while Abramoff worked at Preston Gates and then at Greenberg Traurig, the center received a few large donations from different Abramoff clients, including the Mississippi Choctaws, and then Ridenour used her center to forward the money to Abramoff and Scanlon for projects that they were trying to conceal. Founded in 1982, Ridenour's center had an established conservative pedigree.

According to Ridenour, who testified before the Indian Affairs panel in mid-2005, she invited Abramoff to join her board in the fall of 1997. The invitation came just a couple of months after her group, with Abramoff's fund-raising help, sponsored the August 1997 trip to Moscow for DeLay and several of his top staffers, including Buckham. During the next seven years, Abramoff seemed to enjoy special status: his word was usually taken at face value, and he exploited his position for his own ends, according to Senate testimony and documents. Ridenour portrayed herself as someone who fully trusted Abramoff's integrity, but at times she sounded remarkably vague and naïve when describing his role as a board member where he wore several different hats and exercised considerable influence.

In some cases, Ridenour's eagerness to help Abramoff was palpable, and he exploited it fully, according to some e-mails released by McCain's committee. Abramoff, for example, told a colleague in a September 2002 e-mail that he could quietly ship $500,000 from one of his clients to the center, boasting that the think tank "can direct money at our discretion, anywhere if you know what I mean." Later that morning, Abramoff sent an e-mail to Ridenour, informing her that "I might have $500K for you to run through NCPPR. Is this still something you want to do?" Ridenour seemed delighted. "Yes we would love to do it," she replied in an e-mail back to Abramoff. In October of 2002, the center received its largest donation ever, a check for $1 million from the Mississippi Choctaws, which Abramoff had arranged. Shortly after the check arrived, the center sent out three checks at Abramoff's behest. One check for $450,000 went to Abramoff's own Capital Athletic Foundation, another for $500,000 went to Scanlon's Capitol Campaign Strategies, and a third for $50,000 was sent to Nurnberger & Associates, which turned out, according to records, to be a debt of Abramoff's that the center helped repay.

During her Senate testimony, Ridenour was pressed about the $1 million donation by the Choctaws. Noting that Abramoff had told the tribe that the donation would be used for "grassroots" activities to influence legislation, McCain asked Ridenour, "Did he tell you this?" Ridenour responded, "Not only did he not tell me that he repeatedly told me that legislation would not be involved."

But later when questioned further by Senator Dorgan, Ridenour conceded that she never actually received an invoice from Abramoff's foundation for his "grant" but instead got one from Greenberg Traurig that indicated the grant request was for a "sports and politics" project. Dorgan also pointed out to a somewhat embarrassed Ridenour that a project involving politics could jeopardize her group's tax-exempt status.

Ultimately, Ridenour acknowledged that her group's controls and oversight of Abramoff had been lax. "We did not receive a formal grant proposal and I assure you in the future we certainly will," Ridenour testified somewhat sheepishly. Similarly, at Abramoff's behest, Ridenour also paid a very large consulting fee of $1.28 million to Kay Gold, an Abramoff-run company that received many millions in Gimme Five kickbacks from Scanlon. Ridenour told the Senate panel that Abramoff had misled her about Kay Gold's true nature by describing it as a Scanlon-run firm.

A similar laxity toward Abramoff's conduct and coziness with his wheeling and dealing seems to have been displayed by Rabbi Daniel Lapin, the leader of the Seattle-based Toward Tradition, the influential conservative Jewish group instrumental in forging ties between Orthodox Jewry and evangelical Christian groups and their leaders. In his plea bargain, Abramoff acknowledged that he had arranged for $50,000 to be sent to a consulting company run by Lisa Rudy, the wife of DeLay's then deputy chief of staff Tony Rudy, in exchange for Rudy's legislative help on two issues. Those funds came from two Abramoff clients, eLottery and the Magazine Publishers of America, both of which Rudy and DeLay helped, but were paid to Toward Tradition. The charity, in turn, hired Lisa Rudy to organize a Washington conference for the nonprofit. Lapin initially went to great lengths after Abramoff's plea bargain to defend his group's integrity from charges that the lobbyist, a longtime board member, had done anything improper. In an interview with a local Seattle paper, Lapin explained that Abramoff came to him in mid-2000 to ask if the group had picked anyone yet to help handle an upcoming conference in Washington. When the lobbyist was told that the job was still open, he quickly stated that he knew just the person and could arrange for her salary to be covered as well. At that point, Lapin recalled, he gave Abramoff the go-ahead.

Lapin continued to maintain that Lisa Rudy did a good job in helping organize the conference. But as the fallout from Abramoff's plea spread wider, Lapin began slowly to distance himself a bit from his old friend. Lapin, who calls himself an opponent of gambling, in a letter to his board in early 2006 belatedly and rather awkwardly raised questions about why eLottery had sent $25,000 to fund his organization in the first place. Lapin reflected that "now we are told that it was at Jack Abramoff's direction and that he had purposes that went beyond helping Toward Tradition."

Lapin's laxness toward Abramoff's behavior seems to have been endemic. Notably, Abramoff wrote a wacky e-mail to Lapin about his need for some awards or honors to help him gain membership to Washington's exclusive and tony Cosmos Club, a request that elicited a quick and friendly response. Abramoff apologized for bothering Lapin with "something so silly" but explained that "most prospective members have received awards and I have received none. I was wondering if you thought it possible that I could put that I have received an award from Toward Tradition with a sufficiently academic title, perhaps something like scholar of Talmudic Studies?" Lapin seemed all too willing to oblige. In an e-mail back, Lapin offered Abramoff a big "Mazel Tov . . . The Cosmos Club is a big deal . . . I just need to know what needs to be produced . . . letters? plaques? Neither?"

When the e-mails made national news and became fodder for late-night comedians in the summer of 2005, Lapin tried gamely to say that he was only joking and also suggested that Abramoff too was merely fooling around, a notion that, judging by Abramoff's past behavior, seems unlikely.

EIGHT

Endgame

∎

By early 2004, Abramoff was getting jittery as his casino lobbying empire began to crumble. For all his ability to keep one step ahead of serious trouble, Abramoff had good reason to be worried. *The Washington Post*, he had learned, was working hard on a big story about the tens of millions that Abramoff and Scanlon had been paid by four casino-rich tribes. Abramoff knew that the exposé would contain other unpleasant revelations and feared that it might disclose parts of his still secret dealings with Scanlon. He decided to give a heads-up to Norquist.

On Friday afternoon, February 20, two days before the story hit, Abramoff sent a quick e-mail to Norquist to tip him off about the impending bombshell, while trying to make light of it too. "FYI, the Post is going to do a major hit on me, probably coming this weekend. It's on our tribal representations. Oh well, I guess I won't be welcome at the ACLU meetings any longer."

Abramoff's sense of foreboding was justified: other reporters had already started to dig into his lucrative business and raise damaging questions. In September of 2003, a tiny paper in Alexandria, Louisiana, called *The Town Talk* had uncovered some financial dirt involving the Coushattas and Abramoff and

Scanlon. The paper had reported, among other things, that in 2002 alone the tribe had paid $13.7 million to Scanlon with virtually no records of what he did for all that money. Likewise, other spending on Abramoff and Scanlon couldn't be accounted for adequately and tribal leaders were squabbling with each other over where all the money went and who was responsible.

Not long after the *Town Talk* story came out, Abramoff's associate Kevin Ring picked up hints that Abramoff and Scanlon had a secret kickback deal going. It didn't take long for Ring to see much bigger trouble ahead. Prophetically, Ring told one of his colleagues, "This could be the Enron of lobbying."

The *Post* piece ran on page 1 on Sunday, February 22, and it carried a big wallop, confirming Ring's prediction about the cataclysm ahead. Written by Susan Schmidt, one of the paper's star investigative reporters, the story documented for the first time how since early 2001 four tribes had paid the two influence merchants at least $46 million for their services. The article also pointed out that Abramoff was charging the tribes as much as $180,000 a month, a rate that was ten to twenty times what some of the tribes' ex-lobbyists had been getting. Greenberg Traurig had pulled in a total of about $15 million, but the bulk of the funds Schmidt revealed went to Scanlon's little-known Capitol Campaign Strategies, which didn't have to publicly disclose them. The story quoted Bernie Sprague of the Saginaw Chippewas' council, who had recently spearheaded a successful drive to kill Abramoff's and Scanlon's contracts because of concern that the two had vastly overstated economic and political threats and grossly overcharged the tribe. "Tribes are gullible," he told the *Post*.

The story revealed that tribal funds had flowed to several conservative groups that seemingly had almost nothing to do with Indian issues, such as Federici's Council of Republicans for Environmental Advocacy and Norquist's Americans for Tax Reform. Schmidt noted that Scanlon had bought a lavish $4.7 million waterfront mansion in Rehoboth Beach and had rented a $17,000-a-month apartment in Washington at the Ritz-Carlton.

Finally, Schmidt, who had been tipped off by rival lobbyists to some of the humongous fees that Abramoff's clients were paying him, reported that the FBI had launched probes into money spent for the lobbying by the Coushattas and the Saginaw Chippewas. Both Abramoff and Scanlon vigorously defended their work—but in very broad strokes—as did some of their tribal backers. But the piece didn't reveal the kickback scheme that the two men had worked out, and Abramoff flatly denied to Schmidt that he had any financial ties with Scanlon.

Several of Abramoff's lobbying associates read the story on-line late Saturday night and early Sunday morning and were busily e-mailing commentary and quips back and forth. Kevin Ring, who got up from bed and read the story, responded to an e-mail from Neil Volz, Ney's former chief of staff, about the likely fallout. "Lots of damning facts in there," Ring wrote. "To be very honest, the Scanlon stuff makes me sick to my stomach—buying property in cash. I am glad she did not no [sic] more about the AIC [American International Center] but the firm does."

Ring forwarded the e-mail to his friend Matt DeMazza, whom he quickly filled in on some of the background to the story and revealed more details of the scam. "Firm is losing clients because of Scanlon. Firm doesn't appreciate that. I expect corrective action by the firm or something will have to give."

The day after the story broke, the mood at Greenberg Traurig was grim. But Abramoff gamely tried to downplay and spin the story. Around half past eight on Monday morning, Abramoff started to e-mail clients and friends an electronic copy of the story, which he called a "hit piece," and quickly tried to put the best face on things. "The reporter was a real racist and bigot," Abramoff wrote in one e-mail. At 11:05 a.m. Tigua consultant Marc Schwartz responded, "Well, it wasn't pretty. It sure looks like Scanlon was living a little large, huh! Call me when you get a chance." Two minutes later Abramoff responded, "Don't you love Washington? I'll try to call you later today."

But Abramoff's team started to tell their boss that he needed to take action. At 12:30 p.m. Monday, Todd Boulanger, one of Abramoff's closest buddies at the firm, whose wife, Jessica, worked for Majority Whip Roy Blunt of Missouri, sent Abramoff an e-mail that called for action and conveyed a sense of urgency. "Well you need to know that all the leadership press people (our friends) think we need to do something. Like op eds from our clients saying they get what they pay for also, delay's office is not happy with this article AT ALL. They are considering issuing a statement that says Scanlon is not an ally or friend of the office . . . you don't want people to start linking you guys together . . . something needs to be done jack. DO NOT SHARE THIS WITH MIKE." Abramoff responded immediately: "I won't share it with anyone. We need to strike back with letters from the tribes. We need to organize this internally and quickly. Where are you now? Can we chat?"

Fallout came fast that day on Capitol Hill. McCain, the chairman of the Senate Commerce Committee and the second-ranking GOP member on the Indian Affairs Committee, called in his top investigative counsel, Pablo Carrillo. A New Orleans native and a graduate of Tulane Law School, Carrillo had earned a reputation as a relentless investigator. An intense man in his early thirties with a hearty laugh, Carrillo had spent much of 2003 delving into a defense scandal involving a $23.5 billion deal for Boeing to supply one hundred refueling aircraft to the Air Force.

When Carrillo came into McCain's office that Monday, the senator dropped a copy of Schmidt's *Post* story on his desk and gave Carrillo new marching orders. "Hey, boy, here's your next project," he said with a mischievous smile, according to a source familiar with the encounter. It was only a matter of a couple of weeks before the first subpoenas went out for documents; and Carrillo quickly recruited a second top-notch counsel and investigator named Bryan Parker, whom he knew from their undergraduate years at Tulane. Moreover, McCain quickly worked out a special arrangement with the then chairman of Indian Affairs, Senator Ben Nighthorse Campbell of Colorado, to conduct the hearings jointly, an arrangement that lasted through 2004 until Campbell retired and McCain became the panel's chairman.

The pressures were mounting on Abramoff and his team to act. Within days, Abramoff had launched a counteroffensive to contain the damage to their images and business. One strategy was to get statements from a few tribal clients and allies attesting to Abramoff's good work and attacking the *Post* story. Letters were drafted by one of Abramoff's associates, one of which was signed by Saginaw Chippewa council member and former chief Maynard Kahgegab Jr., who remained a strong ally. But Kahgegab's views were now in the minority on the tribal council. In late 2003, new council elections were held, which brought in a new chief in Audrey Falcon and some other new leaders. Shortly thereafter, Abramoff and Scanlon were sacked.

Abramoff had even taken some preemptive action with the Coushattas about ten days before the *Post* story ran. In one early strike to shore up his Coushatta power base, Abramoff had reached out to Steve Griles at Interior for help just before the story came out. Abramoff had pressed Griles to get BIA to send a letter that affirmed that Lovelin Poncho was still the chairman of the Coushattas. The letter was significant because the Coushattas were going through a bitter internal struggle between critics of Abramoff and loyalists, and having BIA weigh in bolstered Abramoff's allies at a difficult moment.

The next salvo was a letter sent to John McCain from William Worfel, who was still on the Coushatta council and continued to back Abramoff. Dated March 1, Worfel's two-page letter disputed some of the *Post* story's facts and its tone. Worfel wrote that he wanted to alert McCain to the "clearly anti Indian slant [in the story] and to suggest to you that a hearing on the issues raised in the article will likely be viewed as an attack on tribal sovereignty." Worfel also called the article's depiction of Greenberg Traurig and Capitol Campaign Strategies "completely unfair and unwarranted."

But Worfel's adamant defense of Abramoff and Scanlon's tribal work had melted away by 2005. "In my mind, they're educated thieves who must be brought to justice," he told the Indian Affairs panel.

Things were moving quickly on other fronts too. Near the top of Abramoff's list of worries was what impact the news would have on his ties to DeLay's office. Right after Schmidt's article, DeLay started to get deluged with questions from reporters about his ties to Abramoff and Scanlon, and he quickly tried to downplay his relationships and distance himself from them. "What I can tell you is that if anybody is trading on my name to get clients or to make money, that is wrong and they should stop it immediately," DeLay told a group of reporters on Capitol Hill on February 24.

In turn, Abramoff tried to reach out to DeLay by dashing off an e-mail to the congressman's wife a few days later. On March 2, he tried to allay her fears about the story. "I am sorry I have not been in touch in the past week or so to let you know that Tom and you are in my prayers," Abramoff wrote. "You are so very much. Unfortunately, for me I too am under a horrific assault by a combination of leftists, jealous lobbyists and renegade mem-

bers of tribes who do not like what we have done with them politically . . . I take great strength and solace in reading Job on the
Sabbath . . . I need a great deal of it today—as my own firm is
leaving me twisting a bit in the wind. I hope I am reading it
wrong . . . May G-D's countenance shine on us all as we weather
the latest salvos. Warmest regards, Jack."

Abramoff was right on the money, though he could have
been more forthcoming with DeLay's wife. According to
former lobbying colleagues, at the very time the embattled lobbyist was tapping out his note, three senior members of the
management team at Greenberg Traurig arrived unannounced in
Washington—two from Florida and one from New York—for a
final showdown with Abramoff and were trying to locate him.
Shana Tesler, who worked closely with Abramoff on some personal projects like Signatures, was trying to reach him and asking other lobbyists if they could help.

Eventually, after lunch, the meeting took place and Abramoff
was told he had to go. In a brief press release, Greenberg Traurig stated that it had recently learned details about some of
Abramoff's "personal transactions and related conduct that were
unacceptable to the firm." Those transactions had actually been
disclosed a few days earlier at the Greenberg Traurig office in
Florida, where Abramoff was asked pointedly about his financial
ties with Scanlon. In response, the lobbyist falsely informed top
management that he had received only $10 million, instead of
over $20 million, in kickbacks from Scanlon. At the meeting,
sources say that at one point Abramoff, in trying to defend himself, started to cry. In self-defense, Abramoff maintained that
much of what he'd ripped off in kickbacks went to the Eshkol
Academy.

Calling the firm's action "regrettable," Abramoff tried to spin
his ouster. He publicly referred to "our mutual decision to ensure that recent events did not interfere with the representation
of our clients." In mid-March 2004, when I did a telephone in-

terview with Abramoff, he told me that he was proud of his work and thought that "any objective analysis of the work we did couldn't but reach the conclusion that our work was immensely beneficial" for the tribes. Within days, Abramoff and a few of his lobbying team, including Boulanger, moved to Cassidy & Associates, one of Washington's largest lobbying firms, with a small amount of their business. While Boulanger and a couple of other Abramoff associates were brought into Cassidy as full-time lobbyists, Abramoff was made an outside consultant who was supposed to rope in new business, a relationship that proved short-lived. In the months after Abramoff was ousted, Greenberg Traurig moved to repair its image and worked out confidential financial settlements with several of the tribes that Abramoff represented, including the Tiguas, the Saginaw Chippewas, the Mississippi Choctaws, and the Agua Caliente. According to sources familiar with these settlements, the payments to the tribes averaged about $10 million each and, in some cases, gave the firm the right to pursue future legal claims against Abramoff. One of the tribes, the Choctaws, posted a statement on its Web site, noting that the firm had "acted honorably." The tribe also indicated that the settlement "fully and fairly resolves all of the tribe's claims for recovery of funds arising from Mr. Abramoff's misconduct." One other tribal client, the Louisiana Coushattas, has filed a suit against Greenberg Traurig that was still in the courts.

Meanwhile, an extensive investigative and legal apparatus soon went into action on Capitol Hill, at a federal interagency task force led by Justice, and in the media—all focused on Abramoff and Scanlon's Indian casino work. For the next two years, several probes would be in operation, with the Justice investigation also looking into other parts of Abramoff's influence-peddling operations for some domestic and foreign clients.

Much of the investigative momentum came from the Senate probe. McCain is a longtime champion of campaign finance and lobbying reforms, and his probe into Indian casinos was tailor-made for the maverick, but in many ways conservative, senator. McCain had spent years spearheading legislation to close the "soft money" loophole in campaign-spending laws. That effort had been an uphill battle. But finally in 2002, Congress enacted a bill that curbed the ability of corporations, individuals, and unions to give tens of millions of dollars to political party committees to use for television ads and get-out-the-vote drives at election time.

But McCain's mammoth investigation required a different kind of stamina, which the Senate panel and its leader displayed in spades. To be sure, the inquiry also afforded McCain a juicy opportunity to take on old foes: Abramoff had worked with Ralph Reed in mounting a multi-million dollar blitz that helped defeat McCain in the pivotal South Carolina primary in the 2000 presidential race. And the lengthy probe also gave McCain another chance to burnish his reformer credentials. McCain had long tried to erase the memory of the Keating Five Scandal; he was one of five Senators who famously met with regulators in 1987 on behalf of the Arizona S&L kingpin.

During the course of the Indian Affairs probe, the committee held five hearings in the Hart Senate Office Building. The sessions, which usually lasted a few hours each and were packed with reporters, lobbyists, criminal lawyers, and tribal representatives in the audience, painted a damaging portrait of how the two influence merchants pulled off many of their heists.

At separate hearings, both Abramoff and Scanlon "took the Fifth" and declined repeatedly to answer questions posed by senators. Looking back on the probe, McCain said it combined elements of "high tragedy with farce." The tragedy in McCain's eyes included blatant lies by Abramoff and Scanlon denying that they had financial ties, grossly inflated fees, and other scams aimed at bilking tribes of their new casino wealth. "The Indians were the most exploitable because they were the most naïve,"

McCain told me in an interview in his office one winter day in early 2006. The senator recalled that Scanlon had billed a few of the tribes millions each to assemble research databases of vendors and other potential supporters that were actually worth about $100,000 apiece. "You could probably get it out of a phone book," the senator quipped. "They were totally exploited."

The farce, in McCain's view, was poignant. With a sly grin playing across his face, the senator recalled testimony about how the tribes paid humongous sums for skyboxes. "You can't make it up. The Indians would pay hundreds of thousands of dollars for skyboxes at Redskins games."

McCain recalled that when the investigation started, he had "no idea of the magnitude of this thing and the brazenness of it. It is style and substance. The substance was shocking, but the style was also—the demeaning of the Indians. People were really affected by that. You rip them off and then you call them 'troglodytes' and 'idiots.'"

It's hardly surprising that the lengthy probe had its share of obstacles. A key hurdle in the early stages was convincing all the tribes to cooperate. Initially, the Choctaws and the Coushattas were reluctant, for different reasons. In both cases, the tribes had to be won over through delicate negotiation and shown deference to alleviate tribal concerns about sovereignty.

During the course of its two-year investigation, the committee issued more than seventy subpoenas and other requests for documents and received over 750,000 pages of records. But arguably the richest detail the panel obtained was buried in the thousands of e-mails between Abramoff and his colleagues, which proved crucial in piecing together the story of how the tribes were defrauded. From the first, the e-mails provided insight into the character and modus operandi of Abramoff and Scanlon. "The e-mails were indispensable," one Senate prober told me. "They not only gave us a shortcut in discovering what was done, but what the intent likely was. This is the kind of information one ordinarily gets from doing scores of discovery. The intent to deceive the tribes was certainly reflected in the e-mails." The e-mails came in fast and furious after the committee issued an early subpoena to Greenberg Traurig.

Ironically, Abramoff may have inadvertently been instrumental in helping the committee and Justice make its case. "Jack had been such a prima donna at Greenberg Traurig that he raised a big stink whenever he got a new laptop," a source familiar with the investigation told me. "As a result, the IT folks at Greenberg had burned [copied] all his e-mails."

To be sure, Abramoff's voluminous e-mail trail and the Senate committee's work proved very helpful to the federal criminal probe as well. While the Senate probe was making headlines, the Justice-led investigation was also quietly but steadily making headway. The federal task force that had been mobilized was a large one. Under the leadership of the Justice Department's Public Integrity and Fraud sections, the task force boasted some three dozen FBI agents and investigators as well as representatives from Interior and the Internal Revenue Service.

The public corruption piece was spearheaded by Mary Butler, a longtime prosecutor with a reputation for diligence and fairness. A graduate of Vassar and the University of Wisconsin Law School, Butler is extremely thorough and meticulous in building cases against public officials. Josh Berman, a Washington lawyer in private practice who worked for two years at Public Integrity with Butler, calls her style "incredibly methodical. Some prosecutors rely heavily on their agents. My guess is that she's looked at every single phone record, credit card receipt, bank record, and plane ticket to Scotland." Berman told me that "she's superpleasant and funny when she wants to be, but she's tough when she needs to be." Before joining Public Integrity in the late 1990s, Butler had been in private practice in Chicago and had spent about twelve years in the U.S. Attorney's Office in

South Florida prosecuting corruption and white-collar cases. Butler also worked briefly for the independent counsel's office in its eighteen-month probe of former interior secretary Bruce Babbitt, who served under President Bill Clinton and was eventually cleared.

To longtime observers of corruption cases, the federal task force that Butler helped run in Washington was run by the book. "It appears that the investigation has proceeded in a classic fashion," Randall Eliason, a former chief of the Public Corruption Section for the U.S. Attorney's Office in the District of Columbia, explained to me. "They've been working their way up the ladder. These white-collar cases take a long time." Eliason also pointed out that this kind of case tends to be "document intensive" and that key witnesses typically have good and expensive attorneys, both factors that can make such cases extremely time-consuming.

The Washington case seemed to gain momentum from Abramoff's earlier legal headaches in SunCruz. A federal grand jury had been impaneled in Florida in 2002 to look into allegations of fraud involving the $23 million wire transfer that Kidan and Abramoff used to secure loans for their acquisition of SunCruz. In April 2003 the 11th Circuit Court of Appeals ruled that the settlement that Abramoff and Kidan struck with the Boulis estate in 2001 was fraudulent and should never have been allowed by the bankruptcy judge. In making its ruling, the court stated that Kidan's management of the floating casinos was "riddled with fraudulent and dishonest transactions."

On August 11, 2005, while Abramoff and his twelve-year-old daughter were on vacation in Los Angeles, the federal grand jury in Florida returned a six-count indictment against Abramoff and Kidan, charging them with wire fraud and conspiracy in their acquisition of SunCruz casinos. The lobbyist was arrested that same day in Los Angeles. By contrast, Kidan was allowed to turn himself in a day later in Florida. The indictment against both men meant that each of them could face as much as thirty years in jail, since every count carried a penalty of up to five years. Both Kidan and Abramoff also faced fines of up to $250,000 per count.

The charges had other significance for the federal case under way in Washington: they added to the pressure on Abramoff to cooperate with prosecutors, whom he'd already been in discussion with for several months. With Abramoff facing real jail time in Florida, former prosecutor Eliason suggested that the lobbyist was "hoping to help himself in Florida by cooperating in D.C."

Roughly a month later, the federal criminal probe netted its first target. On Friday, September 16, Justice charged that David Safavian, a former chief of staff at the General Services Administration, had lied to federal investigators about not having business dealings at GSA with Abramoff prior to their Scotland junket with Ney in 2002. Safavian, an old friend of Abramoff's who had worked briefly as a lobbyist with him at Preston Gates, had allegedly misled first GSA officials and then federal investigators by asserting that he and Abramoff had not had lobbying contacts in the run-up to the trip, according to the indictment. Safavian, who in early 2004 had become chief procurement officer for the White House's Office of Management and Budget, resigned from his job at once. A few days later he was arrested at his home in suburban Virginia.

In its indictment on October 5, 2005, Justice indicated that in the weeks immediately before the Scotland trip, Abramoff and Safavian had been e-mailing each other furiously. According to e-mails that were released by Justice, Abramoff was lobbying his old colleague to obtain leases on two government properties in the Washington area. Abramoff asked Safavian for his help in leasing forty acres of land in White Oak, Maryland, which the lobbyist envisioned as a new home for the Eshkol Academy.

Abramoff was also pressing Safavian for assistance in leasing the Old Post Office Building in Washington, which Abramoff was eyeing as a hotel development project with at least one tribal client, the Chitimachas of Louisiana.

The e-mail trail surely grabbed the attention of investigators. In one revealing exchange shortly before the trip, Abramoff was asked by a lobbying associate why he was focusing so much on Safavian and the upcoming trip. "Why Dave? I like him but didn't know u did as much. Business angle?" his colleague wondered. Abramoff quickly replied, "Total business angle. He is new COS of GSA."

In mid-April, just about a month before the trial of Savafian got under way, Justice released another batch of 278 e-mails that further highlighted what one prosecutor described as a "highly inappropriate relationship" between Abramoff and Safavian. These e-mails painted a picture of a close relationship that Abramoff was exploiting to gain Safavian's help. In an e-mail exchange in late July 2002, just prior to the Scotland trip, Abramoff showed his eagerness to get together more with Safavian: "Golf Friday? Golf Sunday? Golf Monday? Golf, golf, golf!" Other records reveal that just days before the trip took place, Safavian and another GSA official had a meeting with Pam Abramoff to discuss the project. According to one e-mail, Safavian even suggested that Abramoff advise his wife to use her maiden name at the meeting to lessen the risks that other agency officials might link her with Abramoff, whom he was trying to help as quietly as possible.

But Safavian's attorney, Barbara Van Gelder, a former federal prosecutor, repeatedly questioned the Justice e-mail dumps in the run-up to the trial. She consistently told reporters that her client was innocent and was being squeezed by the Justice Department for information in what she portrayed as a kind of fishing expedition.

Justice was moving aggressively on other fronts in the Abramoff probe to catch bigger fish. On a rainy and blustery day in late November 2005 at the federal district court in Washington, a well-tanned Michael Scanlon pleaded guilty to one count of fraud and bribery and agreed to pay restitution of $19.7 million to four tribes. Under the terms of the deal, Scanlon agreed to cooperate with the ongoing corruption probe and testify against Abramoff and public officials. The once high-flying spin man faced a maximum sentence of five years in jail.

In his plea bargain, Scanlon stated that he had conspired with Abramoff to defraud four tribes of $19.7 million in a kickback scheme. The plea deal also referred to a conspiracy to bribe public officials and mentioned an unnamed representative and senior staff member. The Justice document said that the two officials had accepted a "stream of things of value," including a golf junket to Scotland, meals at an upscale restaurant in Washington, and other financial perks, in exchange for their help in Congress. The representative, according to the plea, helped by putting statements in the *Congressional Record* to facilitate the SunCruz deal for Abramoff and promised to introduce a measure that would reopen casinos for two Texas tribes. Essentially, Scanlon had implicated and agreed to testify against Bob Ney and Neil Volz, his ex–chief of staff.

A spokesman for Ney maintained that the congressman was innocent of any wrongdoing. "Any allegation that Representative Ney did anything illegal or improper is false," Brian Walsh said.

In his brief afternoon court appearance, Scanlon spoke softly and answered questions from Judge Ellen Segal Huvelle with simple yes and no replies. But once he left the court, Scanlon seemed to revert to his old grandstanding style with the press as he chatted up a few friends in the crowd and wore a big, somewhat goofy grin. When asked by one reporter why he looked so happy, Scanlon could only respond, "I'm always smiling." Scanlon also joked with several reporters that he would be seeing them around.

For all his bluster, Scanlon was at a loss for words when asked whether he wanted to express any regrets to the tribes. After an awkward silence of about ten seconds, Plato Cacheris, Scanlon's high-priced attorney, offered a quick apology of sorts. Scanlon "was regretful for what happened to the tribes, but he has nothing to say now," Cacheris told reporters outside the court in an impromptu press conference.

The Scanlon plea was followed quickly by a December plea in Florida by Adam Kidan in the SunCruz case. Kidan's plea acknowledged that he and Abramoff had committed fraud in the purchase of the floating casino operation in 2000; it also meant that Kidan was prepared to testify against Abramoff in their upcoming trial. Together, Kidan's and Scanlon's separate pleas were the equivalent of a pincer attack on Abramoff. Both of the deals implicated Abramoff in criminal conspiracies and greatly increased the pressures on the beleaguered lobbyist to quickly cut his own deals, not just in Washington but also in Florida, where his SunCruz trial was set to begin on January 9, 2006.

Moreover, Abramoff had been telling friends for months that he was running out of money, a circumstance that seemed plausible. Signatures, which Abramoff finally closed in the fall of 2005, after he was unable to sell it, had long been a big financial drain, and his legal bills were easily running $1 million a year. Since early 2004, Abramoff had been paying for the services of two expensive white-collar attorneys. To handle the federal probe in Washington, Abramoff had retained Abbe Lowell, a high-powered criminal lawyer whose previous clients included former representative Gary Condit, and in Miami, Abramoff was using Neal Sonnett, a prominent criminal lawyer, to work the SunCruz case.

By late 2005, anxiety levels on Capitol Hill and K Street

about a possible Abramoff plea deal were high. On the morning of January 3, 2006, a small army of reporters and television camera crews gathered early to get choice spots to view Abramoff as he entered and exited U.S. District Court for the District of Columbia on Constitution Avenue. Inside the courtroom, Abramoff appeared ashen and looked downcast during his plea hearing before Judge Huvelle. The onetime überlobbyist pleaded guilty to fraud, tax evasion, and conspiracy to bribe public officials and agreed to pay restitution of $25 million—mostly to four tribes plus $1.7 million in back taxes.

In his plea agreement, Abramoff implicated Ney and Volz for taking bribes in exchange for their help with a few clients and other business projects, including the Tiguas and SunCruz. Abramoff also added new bribery allegations against Tony Rudy, the former deputy chief of staff to DeLay who had become his lobbying associate at Greenberg Traurig. Rudy, though not mentioned by name, was accused of accepting $86,000 in illegal payments, most of which was funneled by two Abramoff clients through a nonprofit to a consulting firm created by Lisa Rudy. In exchange, Rudy had provided help in 2000 in quashing two bills, one of which was the Internet gaming bill that Abramoff's client eLottery had wanted killed. In his plea bargain, Abramoff confessed to defrauding Greenberg Traurig as well as four Indian tribes. The plea bargain also indicated that Abramoff failed to inform Greenberg or one of his clients, Tyco International, that he controlled a small company called Grassroots Interactive that Tyco, at the lobbyist's behest, paid $1.8 million. Abramoff wound up pocketing about $1.7 million of the fees, according to his plea deal. Greenberg Traurig subsequently repaid Tyco. The plea agreement portrayed Greenberg Traurig as an unwitting victim of Abramoff, which has been what the firm has contended from early March 2004 when it ousted the lobbyist. From all indications, the Justice Department probe into Abramoff's influence peddling wasn't investigating either Greenberg Traurig or Preston Gates & Ellis.

At the conclusion of the hearing, a somber-looking Abramoff asked the judge if he could read a brief statement. "Words can never express my sorrow and profound regret," Abramoff told a hushed courtroom. Photos of Abramoff leaving the court caught him dressed memorably in a black raincoat with matching fedora—images that quickly became material for late-night television comics and writers, some of whom remarked on his resemblance to Hollywood's version of a Mafia don.

A few hours later at a press conference at Justice, Alice Fisher, the head of the Criminal Division, summed up Abramoff's plea and the ongoing investigation in stark terms. "Government officials and government actions are not for sale," she told a group of reporters, vowing that investigators would pursue the case vigorously. In Fisher's view, the corruption detailed in Abramoff's plea agreement has "a devastating impact on the public's trust in government."

The very next day, Abramoff appeared in federal court in Miami and pleaded guilty to charges of conspiracy and wire fraud in the acquisition of SunCruz. In that case, Abramoff and Kidan were both sentenced in late March to five years and ten months in jail, the minimum they could have received under sentencing guidelines. As part of their plea deals, Abramoff and Kidan each agreed to pay $21 million to the two lenders they defrauded. Both men, at the request of Justice Department prosecutors, were allowed to remain free for at least ninety days while they continued to cooperate in the Washington criminal probe.

The back-to-back Abramoff pleas triggered shock waves across Washington. During subsequent weeks a legal and political domino effect was triggered, the likes of which are rare in

Washington. Before the end of the first quarter of 2006, the foundations of DeLay's well-oiled political and money machine had started to collapse. In mid-January, the Alexander Strategy Group, the lucrative blue-chip lobbying shop that symbolized DeLay Inc., announced that it was about to shut its doors. Home to Tony Rudy and Ed Buckham, the firm had been jumpstarted in 1998 by Abramoff, whose clients—including the Marianas, the Choctaws, and Russian energy interests—were instrumental in its creation by sending it close to $1 million in business via Buckham's U.S. Family Network. The official word was that the lobbying shop had been closed due to negative publicity from the scandal. But it was apparent that Buckham and Rudy were being looked at hard by Justice investigators as they homed in on the network of former DeLay aides with whom Abramoff had worked closely to gain legislative favors for his clients.

By late March, Rudy had cut a plea deal with Justice that implicated Buckham in Abramoff's bribery schemes. In his March 31 plea, Rudy acknowledged that he had accepted numerous gifts and favors from Abramoff during his time working in DeLay's office—including two golf junkets, tens of thousands in Abramoff-related payments to his wife's consulting firm, free meals at Washington restaurants, and much more. In exchange, Rudy indicated he had provided critical help to at least two Abramoff clients while he worked on the Hill.

At the time of Rudy's plea it was widely believed by Washington insiders that Buckham, who had worked in conjunction with Abramoff to funnel favors to Rudy, was himself plea-bargaining with prosecutors. The new vulnerability of DeLay Inc. was underscored when Richard Armey, another former House majority leader from Texas turned lobbyist, told *The New York Times* that "Tom DeLay sent Buckham downtown to open shop and set up a branch office on K Street. The whole idea was 'what's in it for us.' That's what I thought at the time, and I've seen nothing in the way they've conducted themselves since then to dissuade me from that point of view."

The political noose around DeLay seemed to be tightening. With two of his former aides striking plea deals, the pressure on the former House majority leader was intensifying. Even though it was far from clear whether Justice would ultimately indict De-Lay, the storm clouds were gathering: the probe was edging ever closer to him, which translated into more political headaches in the upcoming election, where he faced a strong challenger. Additionally, Justice investigators were continuing to scrutinize the three trips that DeLay and Abramoff had taken to Scotland, Moscow, and the Marianas, and assessing whether there were links between these junkets and legislative actions taken by De-Lay. Justice was also trying to determine whether $115,000 in consulting fees Christine DeLay had been paid over a three-year period by Alexander Strategy was connected in any way to Abramoff's clients.

On top of all these pressures, DeLay was facing a separate indictment in Texas on charges of laundering campaign contributions and then illegally using them in state races. On April 3, just three days after Rudy's plea, DeLay decided to call it quits. In an announcement that caught many analysts by surprise, De-Lay said he wouldn't be running for reelection and that he would leave Congress before year's end. "I have no fear whatsoever about any investigation into me or my personal or professional activities," DeLay said when he announced his intention to retire after eleven terms.

DeLay may not have been overly concerned about the legal threat that the Abramoff probe posed to his career. But the investigation had exacted a clear emotional and political toll on DeLay, given that top former aides had struck plea deals that ruined their reputations and had at least indirectly tarred DeLay's reputation too. In the end, when DeLay asserted publicly that the Abramoff scandal had "nothing to do" with him and his decision to depart, his words rang hollow.

DeLay's decision to leave Congress wasn't the only development that came in the wake of Rudy's plea agreement. Just five weeks after Rudy's deal, another bombshell in the investigation dropped: Neil Volz reached a long-anticipated plea agreement with Justice, increasing the legal pressures on Bob Ney.

On May 8, the thirty-five-year-old Volz, who had worked for Ney for seven years, including four as his chief of staff, became the third former colleague of Abramoff's to cut a deal with prosecutors to cooperate. Like the others, Volz agreed to testify against the congressman.

Although Ney was not named in the plea, his lawyer Mark Tuohey acknowledged that he was "Representative #1," who was cited in Volz's plea document. The plea alleged that Ney had received a number of favors and gifts from Abramoff and his former chief of staff, including his famous golf junket to Scotland in August 2002, plus trips in 2003 to New Orleans and the Fiesta Bowl in Tempe, Arizona. Volz and Abramoff also showered Ney with free meals and drinks at Signatures and let him use Abramoff's skybox seats at Verizon Center and Camden Yards, according to the agreement.

In its court papers, the Justice Department indicated that in exchange for this "stream of things of value, Volz and his co-conspirators sought and received Representative #1's agreement to perform a series of official acts." In a court document, Volz alleged sixteen separate acts undertaken by Ney to help Abramoff's clients. They included Ney's 2002 promise to introduce a measure to help reopen the Tiguas' Speaking Rock casino; Ney's awarding a lucrative license in 2002 to install antennas for wireless phone service in the House to Foxcom, an Israeli company that later became an Abramoff client at Greenberg Traurig, and which before the contract was awarded gave $50,000 to Abramoff's Capital Athletic Foundation; and Ney's introduction of a measure that would have benefited garment manufacturers in the Northern Marianas, who were fighting efforts to impose U.S. minimum wage laws. Moreover, Volz acknowledged that, like Rudy, he had violated a one-year ban on lobbying his former office on these and other matters.

The conspiracy began when Volz worked for Ney, according to the plea. Volz confessed that when he was in Ney's office, he had received numerous gifts from Abramoff, including free meals, travel, and entertainment, which exceeded the legal gift limit under House rules and which he failed to disclose. In exchange for these favors, Volz took several actions, including persuading Ney to put his two much-publicized statements in the *Congressional Record* in 2000 that facilitated Abramoff's acquisition of SunCruz.

The purpose of the conspiracy involving Volz and Abramoff's other lobbying associates such as Rudy was to "unjustly enrich themselves by corruptly receiving, while public officials, and providing, while lobbyists, a stream of things of value with the intent to influence and reward official acts" by members of Congress.

Volz's cooperation proved to be a key stepping stone in the government's efforts to pursue corruption and eventually persuade Ney to plead guilty. Volz faced a maximum of five years in jail, but wound up with two years of probation, 100 hours of community service, and a $2,000 fine.

Nonetheless soon after Volz's plea, Ney's lawyer Mark Tuohey told reporters in a conference call that Ney's legal team had been talking to federal prosecutors for a few months and that the congressman was willing to "answer any and all questions" from Justice. Tuohey also tried to raise questions about

the accuracy of information that Abramoff and his former colleagues were providing to Justice with regard to Ney: the lawyer
charged that they were "singing for their supper," to lessen their
prison time.

A somewhat beleaguered Ney told Fox News that Abramoff,
Rudy, and Scanlon were trying to stay out of jail and had "said a
lot of things, as I understand, about a lot of people. I think fact
will be separated from fiction . . . I haven't done anything
wrong." When asked if he would resign if he's indicted, Ney said
he wasn't going to "comment on hypotheticals," adding that "I
don't believe I'm going to be indicted." In a statement from his
office, Ney also said, "I have always considered Neil Volz my
friend. I am very saddened to see what happened today."

NINE

The Rules of the Game

■

In the midst of the scandal, both before and after his plea bargain, Abramoff made some stabs at presenting his side of the story, giving interviews to *The New York Times Magazine*, *Time*, and *Vanity Fair*. One of Abramoff's recurring themes in all three venues was that he was being pilloried for activities that are commonplace in the lobbying world. "I can't imagine there's anything I did that other lobbyists didn't do and aren't doing today," Abramoff told *Time*. In a similar vein, Abramoff complained to *Vanity Fair* that he really worked much like others on K Street, only better. "Most Washington lobbyists are lazy, people of limits, people who move glacially slow," Abramoff said. "I felt my job was to go out there and save the world . . . I thought it was immoral to take someone's money and not win for them."

Of course, this is heavily spun stuff, as Abramoff's own plea bargain makes abundantly clear. The lobbyist and his cohorts on Capitol Hill and on K Street subverted norms, ethics, and the law in defrauding Indian casino and other clients out of tens of millions of dollars and conspiring to bribe public officials. Clearly, Abramoff's kickback schemes, bribes to high-level congressional aides, fraudulent use of nonprofits, and other actions were beyond the pale of the lobbying profession at large. The transgressions that Abramoff and his former business associates —Scanlon, Kidan, Rudy, and Volz—have pled guilty to kept prosecutors busy through 2009 and into 2010 as they worked to ferret out how far the corruption schemes went. "Abramoff wasn't just pushing the envelope," quipped Larry Noble, a former counsel at the Federal Election Commission who later ran the Center for Responsive Politics in Washington, a nonpartisan group tracking the influence of money in politics. "He was shredding the envelope."

Nonetheless, there's another way to interpret Abramoff's remarks that reveals some interesting broader truths, not only about the lobbyist's rise and fall but also about the way that Washington works—specifically, how the connections between lobbyists, money, and politicians have tightened considerably over the last decade. In the minds of some former GOP members, the vast and incessant demands of campaign fund-raising in Congress explain many of the political and ethical ills that beset Washington. "Lobbyists are afraid if they don't give, congressmen won't talk to them much," former representative William Frenzel, a Republican from Minnesota who is now with the Brookings Institution, told me. "I think Congress has been merciless in their fund-raising. I think it's a form of extortion. Congress treats the lobbyists as though they're sheep to be fleeced."

Frenzel wasn't talking about the K Street Project directly, though his remarks seem appropos in regard to that operation. The K Street Project owed much to Abramoff, whose extraordinary fund-raising for DeLay and his pet projects, as well as numerous conservative causes, long made him a role model for many conservatives. As Grover Norquist once told *National Journal*, "What the Republicans need is 50 Jack Abramoffs. Then this

becomes a different town." What Norquist and others appreciated so much about Abramoff was that he provided a complete
financial concierge service for his Capitol Hill allies and right-
wing redoubts. Abramoff persuaded his Indian casino clients,
his friends in the Marianas, and other cash cows to part with
millions and millions of dollars—in campaign cash, junkets,
meals, skyboxes, and more—to ingratiate themselves with the
GOP and other power brokers such as Norquist and Reed. In so
doing, Abramoff also of course gained in stature with his friends,
becoming a hero and an indispensable bagman.

The zeitgeist that Abramoff reflected so well was promul-
gated by DeLay and the K Street Project. When the GOP captured Congress in 1994 and in the years directly after, the word
went out from DeLay and Norquist that if you wanted access on
Capitol Hill and if you wanted to have influence with these and
other leaders, you'd better hire Republicans. K Street lobbying
shops and trade groups were told, in no uncertain terms, that
they had to pay more attention to the GOP by hiring more lobbyists from their ranks and upping their contributions to the
party. "We're just following the old adage of punish your enemies
and reward your friends," DeLay famously said of his K Street
strategy to *The Washington Post* not long after the GOP takeover.
"We don't like to deal with people who are trying to kill the revolution. We know who they are. The word is out."

For his part, Norquist could be equally blunt and brutal.
Norquist remarked to Elizabeth Drew for an article in *The New
York Review of Books* in 2005, "There should be as many Demo-
crats on K Street representing corporate America as there are
Republicans in organized labor—and that number is close to
zero."

The GOP effort to establish its own pay-to-play rules and its
own spoils system was, in some respects, an updated, more ag-

gressive, and more far-reaching version of what Democrats had developed when they controlled the House. Back in the 1980s, the Democrats boasted a leading money man in Tony Coelho— a one-time House majority whip and chairman of the Democratic Congressional Campaign Committee. Coelho was brilliantly adept at pressuring lobbyists to fork over more donations to Democrats and well known for calling in chits.

In the GOP remake of the Democrats' political project, Abramoff was one of the early leaders, but he was hardly alone. Trade groups all over Washington felt pressure from the DeLay and Norquist machines to hire more Republicans and, according to surveys, did so overwhelmingly. An official of the Republican National Committee in 2003 was cited in *The Washington Post* observing that all but three of some three dozen top slots at leading business trade groups had been recently filled by Republicans. But sometimes DeLay's heavy-handed tactics provoked ethics storms on the Hill. In late 1998, for instance, DeLay attacked the Electronic Industries Association for having had the temerity to hire former representative Dave McCurdy, an Oklahoma Democrat, rather than a GOP candidate. In response, the House Ethics Committee issued a private letter rebuking the Texan for going too far.

But the reprimand didn't do much to slow down DeLay's hard-driving, push-the-envelope style of remaking K Street, a style that not incidentally benefited Abramoff. A prominent GOP lobbyist with one of the biggest trade groups in Washington told me that he was playing golf with Majority Whip DeLay at one time when he had been taken aback by one of the Texan's suggestions. "Hire Jack Abramoff," DeLay advised after the lobbyist mentioned that he needed extra muscle on an issue. The lobbyist was flummoxed because at the time, he recalled, "I'd never heard of Abramoff." This wasn't the only time that DeLay plugged Abramoff. On their trip to the Marianas over

New Year's in 1998 when DeLay famously and publicly called Abramoff "one of my closest and dearest friends," he also graciously referred to the lobbyist as "your most able representative in Washington."

Abramoff embodied the hard-edged, bullying style of the K Street Project. Abramoff once described his business philosophy to a colleague: "If something is worth doing, its [*sic*] worth overdoing." Young Hill staffers looking for a good time and a hot job in the private sector were drawn to Abramoff. "Jack was good at preying on young boys who had nonworking wives," one GOP lobbyist told me in reflecting on the kinds of staffers Abramoff liked to hire from Congress. One former colleague of Abramoff's put it slightly differently: "Jack created an environment that made a lot of young guys aspire to the same lifestyle."

Besides his flamboyant entertaining and fund-raising, another tool that Abramoff used to great effect in winning the hearts and minds of public officials was his often ostentatious use of religion. Abramoff's Orthodox Judaism had much of the same fervor as the evangelical spirit of Ralph Reed and Ed Buckham, which had been so crucial to the GOP's victory in 1994. What's more, Abramoff's ties to Reed, Buckham, and Rabbi Daniel Lapin, among others, helped nurture an alliance between conservative Christians and like-minded Jews on a range of political issues including their natural interest in strongly backing Israel.

A short thank-you note that Abramoff wrote to Buckham after a golf outing that the two enjoyed together in September 1996 highlights how Abramoff managed to inject a religious note into his lobbying messages. After Abramoff reminded Buckham, then DeLay's chief of staff, about the help he was looking for on a few matters concerning the Mississippi Choctaws and the Marianas, he concluded with a religious flourish that no doubt appealed to Buckham, the lay evangelical minister. Noting that it was the Jewish holiday of Yom Kippur, the Day of Atonement, Abramoff wrote, "Today, all I can do is pray, but, as you know, prayer is really the only important thing that any of us can do. It is all in the hands of Heaven, though we can help move things along, too." Abramoff, Buckham, Reed, and their network of religious conservatives certainly helped move things along for DeLay and others on Capitol Hill and used the casino largesse of Abramoff's clients, as much as prayer, to do so.

Most of the lobbyists who have turned into important money harvesters for congressional leaders are no doubt staying within the legal limits. Nonetheless, several of the lobbying tools—including junkets, free meals, and subsidized sporting events—that Abramoff took to extremes are institutionalized in Washington and are now integral to the ties that bind K Street with Capitol Hill. As editor and journalist Michael Kinsley once remarked about how business in Washington is conducted, "The scandal is not what's illegal. It's what's legal."

The lobbying world has grown rapidly in recent years, and it's easy to see that Abramoff has a point about how other lobbyists and he have a few things in common. It's become standard operating procedure to wine and dine members and staffers away from Washington and to lavishly entertain decision makers on Capitol Hill and at political conventions. Lobbyists have emerged in recent years as chief fund-raisers for many campaigns and leadership PACs.

"It's absolutely true that the amount of money in the lobbying and fund-raising systems has exploded exponentially," said Dirk Van Dongen, president of the National Association of Wholesaler-Distributors and a well-known fund-raiser with good ties to the Bush administration and on Capitol Hill. "I think the underlying cause of all these problems is the amount of money that has to be raised and how it is raised," former senator Warren Rudman, a Republican from New Hampshire, told me in a telephone interview. "By necessity it means going to people who need access, who want to be heard, and who want to influence policy."

Ironically, even as DeLay was stepping down permanently from House leadership early in 2006, the two leading candidates to succeed him were Roy Blunt of Missouri, his top deputy, and John Boehner of Ohio, a longtime rival, both of whom boasted their own sizable networks of Washington lobbyists and fund-raisers. Interestingly in Blunt's case, his outside lobbying allies had strong ties to Buckham's Alexander Strategy Group. Blunt's leadership PAC, Rely on Your Beliefs, long employed Jim Ellis, who was indicted in Texas along with DeLay on money laundering and conspiracy charges and used to run DeLay's ARMPAC too. It's no coincidence that Blunt succeeded DeLay as the House liaison with K Street when DeLay moved up to majority leader in 2002.

For his part, Boehner hosted weekly meetings with top Washington business lobbyists and conservatives for a few years right after the GOP won control of Congress in 1994. The meetings, which became known as Boehner's Thursday Group, were important in garnering the support of the lobbying community for GOP priorities and legislation. Boehner, who like DeLay boasted very strong ties to the tobacco lobby in Washington, once earned notoriety by handing out checks from the industry on the House floor. Boehner's check giveaways to fellow members took place at a sensitive point for the tobacco industry when it was fighting to block attempts to kill a tobacco subsidy.

The struggle between Boehner and Blunt in early 2006 to succeed DeLay—amid calls for lobbying reforms in the wake of the Abramoff scandal—prompted cynical attitudes along the lines of *plus ça change, plus c'est la même chose*. Ultimately,

Boehner won out largely because the ties between Blunt's world and DeLay's seemed more obvious.

But Boehner, who talked tough about lobbying reforms in early 2006, soon backed away from almost all stringent measures to reform the pay-to-play system, as did many of his colleagues in the House. One perk that Boehner was particularly concerned to preserve was the ability of members to take privately funded junkets, not unlike the kind that Abramoff was so good at organizing. According to an independent survey done by the Campaign for a Cleaner Congress, Boehner had taken 180 trips since 1999 outside his district, ranking him among the ten most prolific travelers in the House. The study showed that quite a few of Boehner's trips were to golfing destinations such as St. Andrews in Scotland and Pebble Beach in California.

Boehner's views about the importance of preserving private travel ultimately prevailed with the House leadership. At the start of 2006, House Speaker Dennis Hastert publicly proclaimed that he favored putting "an end" to private travel because of abuses. But the House lobbying reform bill that passed included a much-watered-down provision that only suspended such trips and only until June 15, 2006, a token gesture at best. Similarly, the bill didn't address mounting concerns about the need to tighten the $50 gift and meal limit that lobbyists and members have had to follow for many years.

What's more, Boehner and his colleagues' retreat from demands to curb private travel came in the wake of new data showing that these kinds of trips have proliferated. According to a study by PoliticalMoneyLine in early 2005, some 600 members of Congress since the year 2000 have gone on 5,410 trips that were privately funded at a cost of $16 million. Of that total, $8.8 million were sponsored and paid for by tax-exempt organizations and similar groups that—like the ones that Abramoff used for his junkets—are not required to disclose their funding.

That lack of transparency raised obvious questions about who was really footing the bills, and whether the trips were truly educational or more for pleasure.

The study also found that another $4 million of these trips were being paid for by Washington trade groups and another $2 million by corporations. While lobbyists, law firms, and foreign entities are barred by congressional ethics rules from paying for travel for members and staff, there are no ethics rules curbing business trade groups or nonprofits from doing so directly, a fact many observers of how influence peddling works find strange. In fact, the study found that one of the leading sponsors of member travel during this period was an affiliate of the American Israel Public Affairs Committee, the pro-Israel lobbying behemoth. Another big travel sponsor is the Ripon Educational Fund, an arm of the moderate Republican Ripon Society, which has been jointly run by two lobbyists, former representative Susan Molinari from New York and Richard Kessler, whose clients include several large pharmaceutical companies.

Likewise, Abramoff's prowess at raising big bucks for DeLay's political operations and ARMPAC was part of a broader trend on K Street in the years after the GOP captured Congress: lobbyists, doubling as fund-raisers, became increasingly important to the fortunes of congressional leaders and many other members. According to the Center for Public Integrity, a Washington watchdog group, the number of lobbyists who served as treasurers for members's reelection committees or leadership PACs soared from fifteen in 1998 to seventy-one in the 2004 election cycles.

So-called leadership PACs mushroomed as well and relied heavily on K Street to fuel their growth. Right after the 1994 elections, there were about ninety of these PACs, which raised some $28 million, but by the end of 2004 the number had soared to almost three hundred and they raised $127 million.

These PACs, which are often used to help members win support from their colleagues by handing out thousands of dollars from their war chests to other members in tough races, became so commonplace that many junior members now have them, keeping lobbyists even busier dialing for dollars.

Similarly, the relationships between lobbyists and members have in a number of cases become tighter through the use of earmarks, another tool that Abramoff liked to employ. One of Abramoff's fortes was prodding members of Congress to insert appropriations earmarks into bills quietly, at the last minute and with little scrutiny. A prime example of this was the $3 million school grant that Conrad Burns helped the Saginaw Chippewas obtain. Another variation on earmarking was Ney's pledge to help the Tiguas reopen their casino by adding a measure to the election reform bill in 2002.

During the lobbying reform debates in early 2006, John McCain and other members pointed out that earmarking of pork projects had soared in recent years in areas ranging from defense to highway spending. Representative Jeff Flake of Arizona, another leading GOP critic of earmarks, memorably referred to them as the "currency of corruption." One of the most egregious recent examples of such earmarks was the so-called Bridge to Nowhere, a pet project of two powerful Republicans from Alaska, Senator Ted Stevens and Representative Don Young, that was tucked into the mammoth highway bill without scrutiny and carried a price tag of $223 million. The much-satirized earmark was for a bridge that would link a tiny town of eight thousand with an island that boasted a population of fifty. Overall, according to the Congressional Research Service, earmarks mushroomed from about four thousand a year in the mid-1990s to more than fifteen thousand in 2005. Earmarks, as McCain put it, have "bred lobbyists, which has bred corruption."

The poster boy for the corrupting potential of earmarks was

former representative Randall "Duke" Cunningham of California, who in late 2005 pleaded guilty to accepting some $2.4 million in bribes from defense and other government contractors. In exchange for these extravagant bribes—which included cash, antiques, and yachts—Cunningham helped steer hundreds of millions in defense contracts and other federal business to three defense and technology firms; including MZM Inc. In March of 2006, Cunningham was sentenced to eight years and four months in prison.

Abramoff and Cunningham are "indicative of a broken system that people have taken advantage of," McCain told me. "The number of lobbyists has gone up with the number of earmarks. Duh. There's a direct relationship. We've now reached a point where one lobbyist and one congressman, i.e., Duke Cunningham, are able to get tens of millions of dollars inserted in defense bills and nobody notices." McCain added that there's a particularly insidious quality to the way that some lobbyists and members have played the earmark game. "Campaign contributions coming very close to the time that earmarks are inserted in bills may not meet the technical definition of bribery, but it's the moral equivalent."

Some GOP influence merchants have acknowledged that earmarks have become a big image problem for their lobbying and their party. One GOP lobbyist with strong ties to congressional leaders told me that earmarks spread quickly after his party captured Congress in 1994. "They tried to be purists after the '94 elections, but it didn't last long," the lobbyist said. De-Lay, he added, "realized that you could protect some endangered members with earmarks" by inserting them in key bills for those members who needed to bolster their standing with constituents via juicy pork projects. Another GOP power broker on K Street concurred: "I don't think many of us understood just how corrupting the earmark process is. It became the currency that the leadership used to buy votes. The people who had the votes to give got the joke pretty quickly. When you start to work the linkages on earmarks, it gets rotten pretty quick."

Republicans, to be sure, weren't the only abusers of the earmark process. In April of 2006, *The Wall Street Journal* reported that federal investigators were probing the financial dealings of Alan Mollohan of West Virginia, the ranking Democrat on the House Ethics Committee who also served on the Appropriations Committee. In the latter post, Mollohan reportedly steered some $250 million in earmarked appropriations to five nonprofit groups in his district, one of which was run by a former top aide in his office. The former aide and her husband also purchased $2 million in properties with Mollohan and his wife. Not long after the *Journal* story he stepped down from his post on the Ethics Committee, but Mollohan was later cleared of any misconduct.

With the earmark issue gaining a particularly bad odor in the press and on Capitol Hill, the lobbying reform bill that passed the Senate in late March of 2006 contained a provision that made it harder for members to slip narrowly targeted earmarks into appropriations legislation. The bill also required for the first time that grassroots lobbying—including the kind that Scanlon mastered and exploited—be disclosed. And the measure banned meals paid for by lobbyists and eliminated the ability of members to accept free sports tickets. But overall, the Senate bill focused more on new disclosure measures rather than the tougher enforcement mechanisms that critics like McCain had advocated. In the end, McCain and seven other proponents of tough enforcement voted against the bill because of concerns that it was too weak. The House bill was even weaker than the Senate measure and was derided by most reform groups and editorial writers as a sham.

The result was to be hashed out in a Senate-House conference, but a final bill was never worked out. To many observers the apparent failure of Congress to pass a strong lobbying reform bill was a grim reminder of how Washington works, even in the wake of the Abramoff scandal, which revealed numerous excesses and visible corruption. Other moderate GOP members saw scant prospects for far-reaching lobbying reform anytime soon, with Republicans in control. "For whatever reason, the GOP Congress that got elected in 1994 is not the same Republican Congress of today," Representative Christopher Shays, a Connecticut Republican, told me in early 2006 after the Abramoff plea deal. "We're not a reform-minded Congress. This is a Congress that belittles reforms, that thinks the public doesn't care. We're more like the Democrats of 1994 . . . I think we set out to change Washington, but Washington has changed us."

To some degree, McCain seems to share Shay's sentiment. Reflecting on his investigation and the scandal, McCain voiced a mix of pride and sadness at what has been uncovered. "I'm glad that it's all over," he told me during a forty-five-minute talk in his office in the winter of 2006. "But I'm saddened at what we've uncovered because I believe there's nothing more honorable than public service. When something like this happens, we're all tarred by the brush. I'll bet you that half my constituents, at least, don't know that I was ever involved in this investigation. But they know that I work in a place where there's been a hell of a lot of corruption. So we're all tarred by the brush."

For several Indian casino-owning tribes, the scandal's legacy will be a long one too. Tribal leaders who fought to uncover the frauds committed by Abramoff and Scanlon also express mixed feelings about what they've accomplished and learned through the congressional and federal investigations.

David Sickey of the Coushattas, like several other tribal leaders, feels a sense of pride that the tribes played a big part in exposing the scandal, and he credits McCain with doing a "superb job. It took a lot of courage. He had to know he'd be shedding some negative light on members of Congress."

Sickey also pointed out that tribes have learned that they must "do better due diligence and be more cautious about whom Indian leaders choose to associate with. Indian leaders have learned that there are groups and individuals looking to take advantage of Indian resources. These were painful and expensive lessons."

The tribes, of course, weren't the only ones to experience painful and expensive lessons. The influence-peddling scandal not only left Abramoff's reputation in tatters but also severely damaged the reputations of several members, Bush administration allies, fellow lobbyists, and conservative leaders he long worked closely with and who reaped substantial rewards from his Indian casino clients. While pushing the ethics envelope is not unusual in Washington, a city full of loopholes and lawyers adept at exploiting them, Abramoff's greed, duplicity, and zealousness stand out and will long be remembered.

Epilogue

■

On November 15, 2006, as dawn began to break in the Maryland countryside, Jack Abramoff began a new career—this one as an inmate at the minimum-security federal prison in Cumberland, Maryland. Nestled in the Appalachian Mountains, a stone's throw from the Potomac River, the 334-bed prison had been chosen for primarily one reason: it is only two hours by car from Washington and allowed federal prosecutors and agents easy access to the ex–lobbying kingpin.

Often despondent, Abramoff shared a cell with five inmates (some in on drug charges), ran a bible study group, worked in the prison's kitchen (where he earned less than a dollar an hour), and had regular visits from his wife and friends, including many from the local Jewish community in Silver Spring, where he had such strong ties.

Abramoff has spent scores of hours helping FBI agents and prosecutors comb through records of trips, campaign contributions, free meals, and other particulars of the ongoing probe into his far-flung influence-peddling schemes. By early 2010, the investigation was winding down, but the fallout was far from over. An Abramoff associate and a former Hill aide were both scheduled to go on trial in 2010. Moreover, Michael Scanlon and Tony Rudy were expected to finally be sentenced for their crimes. And finally, and most important to Abramoff, there was the likelihood that he would be released to a halfway house in mid-2010.

The long-running investigation did not surprise Abramoff. After all, in a last e-mail to a number of close friends, hours before he was incarcerated, he had written that "this nightmare has gone on for almost three years so far" and "I expect that we're not even half way through." Abramoff, as it turns out, was prescient. By the end of 2009, twenty ex-lobbyists, Hill aides, Bush administration officials, and one member of Congress had been charged or convicted in the influence-peddling inquiry.

In the months that preceded and followed his imprisonment the scandal's legal and political ramifications were dramatically underscored. Justice notched two of the scandal's biggest convictions shortly before Abramoff was jailed and, soon afterward, several lawmakers were defeated at the polls after intense reelection campaigns in which their close ties to the ex-lobbyist were highlighted. Political shock waves continued as the public's mood toward the lobbying business seemed to darken, due largely to continuing revelations about the scandal's reach and to separate federal inquiries into other lobbying abuses linking earmarks, several prominent Democratic members' and lobbyists' campaign contributions. Efforts to rein in lobbying abuses and excessive influence had accelerated in Congress in 2007, and they continued to do so at the start of the Obama administration.

With all the attention to lobbying abuses, it's logical that the influence business has increasingly been viewed by the public in a negative light. "There's a lot of stuff out there in lobbying and political activity that might look or even be sleazy or unethical, but isn't criminal," Randall Eliason, the former prosecutor, told me. "Campaign contributions followed by official action, on one level, looks like the definition of bribery, but on the other hand is business as usual in Washington."

Ironically, Eliason's view is echoed, after a fashion, by Rep. Dana Rohrabacher (R-Calif.), who describes his longtime friend Abramoff as a "wheeler-dealer" who made some mistakes but operated no differently than many lobbyists. "You have to compare Jack to other lobbyists, not to Mother Teresa," the congressman told me. "He was a wheeler-dealer and I compare him to other wheeler-dealers." Indeed, about the toughest words he has for Abramoff are that his "wheeling and dealing went to his head."

The notion that "business as usual in Washington" often seems sleazy or unethical has been reinforced by the Abramoff scandal and fallout, the last two national elections, and the separate lobbying reforms passed by Congress in 2007 and those adopted by President Obama's administration. Further, the 2006 convictions of David Safavian, the onetime GSA official, and former Rep. Bob Ney of Ohio, offered new insights into Abramoff's lobbying machine and illuminated how the Washington influence business culture has evolved in often-pernicious ways.

Safavian became the first person in the scandal to be convicted by a federal jury. After an eight-day trial in June 2006, Abramoff's former business associate and old friend was found guilty on four counts of making false statements to government officials and obstructing justice in the influence-peddling probe.

While Safavian's trial didn't focus directly on the corruption issues that were at the heart of the Abramoff probe, it provided another useful snapshot of the modus operandi of the influence merchant and his lobbying team. The trial also showcased much damaging testimony by Neil Volz—the former Abramoff associate and onetime top aide to Ney. Volz, who had pleaded guilty earlier in the year, provided incriminating information about Safavian and Ney, the two key guests on the mid-2002 golf junket to Scotland. To get permission to take the golf outing, Safavian had told GSA ethics officials that his contacts with Abramoff were unrelated to official business and claimed that all of Abramoff's lobbying activities were aimed at Capitol Hill.

In his testimony, Volz described Safavian and Ney as "champions" of Abramoff's clients. Volz detailed how Abramoff and his lobbying team reached out to allies in government who "operate at a higher level" and seemed eager to "want to help." At one juncture, Volz said that "David was kind of the brains of the operation," a reference to Safavian's willingness to lend a hand with various projects both before and after the golf junket. Specifically, Volz claimed that both Safavian and Ney provided guidance to Team Abramoff on the property that was being eyed for the Jewish school.

Safavian testified, however, that he believed that the $3,100 he repaid to Abramoff represented the real costs of Safavian's share of the junket. But prosecutors ridiculed Safavian's assertions: they noted that the real costs had to be much higher given the use of a chartered jet, the $500-per-night hotel rooms, the $400 green fees for golf, and the pricey meals and drinks. Under cross-examination by government prosecutors, Safavian acknowledged that he provided Abramoff some "nonpublic information," contrary to what he had initially suggested. Safavian also conceded that he had misinformed FBI agents that he'd only spoken to Abramoff after the Scotland junket about the two government properties the lobbyist was trying to lease. In fact, he testified, he and Abramoff had talked about the properties before the trip. To drive home the point, prosecutors asked Safavian whether he had forgotten some two dozen e-mails that he and the lobbyist had exchanged about the properties in July 2002, just weeks before the junket. In a moment of striking candor, Safavian also referred to Abramoff as a friend and quickly added, "Dare I say it, a mentor."

Although Safavian's conviction was overturned about a year later on appeal, he retried in 2009 and was found guilty on similar charges. In the retrial, Safavian was convicted again on four counts: two of making false statements, one of obstructing an internal GSA investigation, and one of lying on a financial disclosure form. He was acquitted of making false statements to a Senate committee. Safavian faces a one-year jail sentence, which he's expected to start serving in mid-2010.

Ney, meanwhile, pleaded guilty to criminal charges in mid-October 2006. During his court appearance in Washington, he read a written statement in which he apologized for his dealings with Abramoff. The six-term congressman, who had recently spent a month in an alcohol rehabilitation program, said he was "ashamed" that his public service career ended in such a demeaning fashion. "I never acted to enrich myself or get things I shouldn't, but over time I allowed myself to get too comfortable with the way things had been done in Washington, D.C. for too long," Ney said in a court statement.

Plainly, Abramoff and Ney had hit it off. The lobbyist, introducing the congressman to the ways of Washington, steered lots of goodies his way—favors that were well documented in his plea agreement with Justice. Besides the über-junket to Scotland, Ney was treated to lavish excursions in the U.S., taking separate trips to Lake George in New York and to New Orleans: prosecutors valued these three junkets at more than $170,000. Moreover, Abramoff and his associates showered Ney with free meals, sports tickets, and campaign contributions valued at tens of thousands of dollars. In exchange, Ney generously inserted the two statements in the Congressional Record to help boost Abramoff's Sun Cruz acquisition and tried to help get the Tigua casino reopened by inserting provisions in an election reform bill, among other legislative favors. "I accepted things I shouldn't have with the result that Jack Abramoff used my name to advance his own secret schemes of fraud and theft in a way that I never could have imagined," Ney said at his court hearing in 2006.

Notwithstanding Ney's self-criticism, the trial judge opted to add a few months of time to Ney's sentence beyond the Justice recommendation. Ney was sentenced to thirty months in prison, but eventually served just seventeen months before his release in early 2009. Not long afterward, Ney got a job as a talk radio host and he told me in a brief note in late 2009 that he was hoping to write his own book about the scandal's impact.

Others who worked closely with Ney describe the financial and political incentives that made him so eager to do Abramoff's bidding. In the documentary *Casino Jack*, Adam Kidan provides an intriguing account of Abramoff's maneuverings. At first, Kidan, Abramoff's partner in the battle to acquire SunCruz casino, told the filmmaker Alex Gibney that by "sheer coincidence" one of Ney's statements in the Congressional Record touting Kidan's management skills was made on the same day that a $10,000 check was sent by Abramoff's team to the National Republican Congressional Committee on Ney's behalf, to help boost the Ohioan's status with House leaders. Reflecting a bit more on the serendipitous timing, however, Kidan conceded: "I guess you could call this a quid pro quo."

Likewise, Ney's dealings with Abramoff were often driven by the congressman's strong desire to curry favor with former House majority leader Tom DeLay and climb in the House leadership ranks, an effort that seems to have blinded him to the legal and ethical risks. Volz told me that when he traveled with Scanlon in early 2000 to the Marianas Islands to help boost Abramoff's business there, the trip was blessed by Ney, who seemed to have an all-consuming desire to "cultivate relations with DeLay." Abramoff, whom Volz first met in DeLay's office, was plainly considered by Ney to be an important ally in wooing DeLay. "There was no doubt that Bob wanted to climb the ladder of power in the House. If he could help Abramoff's clients while Bob achieved his goals, it was a classic Washington win-win," Volz said.

Volz cooperated in the Justice investigation and received two years' probation. Perhaps more than any other figure in the scandal, Volz has seriously examined his own conduct and the larger implications of Abramoff's influence-peddling operation. He has learned some harsh and very self-critical lessons. "Looking back I realize how important it is to be vigilant in little things because they add up," Volz told me. "It's about a slippery slope," he added, noting that "one little lie leads to another little lie which adds up to a big lie before too long." Ultimately, Volz concluded: "The scandal is about the loss of the public's trust in government. The scandal both fueled and represents the loss of public trust in Washington."

The loss of public trust can translate into election disaster. Just days before Abramoff was jailed, a small electoral tsunami spawned by the scandal hit some of his closest GOP allies in several states as a handful of well-known veterans in the House and Senate lost on election day 2006.

At the top of that list: former Montana Senator Conrad Burns. Burns was linked to Abramoff through some $150,000 in campaign donations that he received from the Abramoff lobbying operation and favors that he did for the lobbyist's clients— such as the $3 million earmark for the Saginaw Chippewas in Michigan—and he was widely reported to be under scrutiny by the Justice Department in the Abramoff investigation. Eventually, Burns was told by Justice in late 2007 or early 2008 that he was no longer being investigated, but by then it was too late. Not long after his defeat in 2006, Burns joined a small Washington lobbying and public affairs firm run by one of his former chiefs of staff. Two congressmen who also benefitted considerably from Abramoff's fundraising largesse, Reps. J.D. Hayworth (R-Ariz.) and Richard Pombo (R-Calif.), both lost their seats. Hayworth was being probed by Justice for many months, according to sources, but the investigation was dropped around the time of the fall elections.

Still more prominent GOP figures were damaged by the scandal's fallout. Abramoff's old friend and covert business associate, Ralph Reed, made his first bid for public office in the 2006 Republican primary for lieutenant governor in Georgia, but voters delivered a stunning verdict. Casey Cagle, a Georgia state senator and Reed's challenger, won the race easily by about 12 percentage points after he spent heavily in the last weeks of the campaign on TV spots that linked Reed to Abramoff. The result was widely seen as a huge blow to the career of Reed, a onetime Georgia GOP chairman who, early on in the race, looked like he would easily snare the nomination.

However, not all of Abramoff's Hill allies met defeat in 2006. Rep. John Doolittle (R-Calif.), whose campaign looked shaky given all his links with Abramoff, managed to survive, albeit in a politically weakened condition. Doolittle's plight only worsened after the FBI raided his suburban home in Virginia seeking further evidence about his wife Julie's lucrative consulting deal with the imprisoned lobbyist. Facing continued Justice scrutiny in 2008, it wasn't surprising that Doolittle opted not to seek re-election that fall.

After the 2006 results were in, some prominent Republicans acknowledged that the Abramoff mess, coupled with other Congressional scandals, helped cost the GOP control of Congress. Even President Bush's top political strategist Karl Rove, who had his own longstanding ties with Abramoff, pointed publicly to the lobbying and congressional scandals as a decisive factor in GOP losses that fall.

Soon after the new Democrat-run Congress convened in early 2007, more political fallout ensued. With their strong campaign rhetoric about the need for ethics and lobbying reforms, the new Democratic leaders moved quickly to assemble and enact a legislative package to make good on their promises by addressing some of the abuses that had been elements of the Abramoff and Duke Cunningham scandals.

In 2007, both Houses passed legislation that made some real changes in the way business is done in Washington, although they failed to address broader concerns about the heavy fundraising burdens on Members that historically have made Congress increasingly dependent on special interests and the lobbying community. Among the key reforms in the legislation were a ban on gifts to members or staff from registered lobbyists or their clients and tougher curbs on travel paid by outside groups and lobbyists. The reform package, known as the Honest Leadership and Open Government Act of 2007, also mandates public disclosure of earmark requests by members, requires lobbyists to provide details of contributions that they have bundled for members, increases the "cooling off" period for members and staff before they can lobby their old offices, and mandates that stealth coalitions identify their donors above $5,000.

The reforms drew a decidedly mixed reception among longtime campaign watchdog groups and lobbyists. Veteran reformer Fred Wertheimer, the head of Democracy 21, applauded several of the new curbs, but also noted that they didn't go far enough. "These reforms did change the relationship between members and lobbyists, but they didn't solve the fundamental problem," Wertheimer told me. Others like Melanie Sloan of CREW, Citizens for Responsibility and Ethics in Washington, are more critical of Congress for not taking an even tougher line, given the dimensions of the Abramoff scandal. In Sloan's view, the reforms were basically "nibbling around the edges," and lacked a real enforcement mechanism.

The naysaying appears justified. Lobbyists, for instance, have managed to circumvent certain new curbs, using conduits to fund junkets, a tool favored by Abramoff that has spread widely in the lobbying community. In the fall of 2009, the *New York Times* reported that, notwithstanding the new curbs on travel, many members were still finding ways of taking junkets using nonprofits and loopholes that appeared at the least to violate the spirit of the new rules and that perhaps broke them.

Nonetheless, for many outside Washington, the scandal highlighted the increasingly symbiotic ties that bind lobbyists to members through fundraising, a business that has grown at Malthusian rates as the costs of campaigns over the last two decades have soared with more and more monies flowing into expensive and often negative television ads. In the 2008, House members who won their races spent an average of more than $1 million on their campaigns, while Senate race winners spent $8.4 million on average, both of which figures are two to three times higher than campaign costs in the mid 1990s. The almost insatiable need of members for more cash has heightened pressures on lobbyists from both parties to keep dialing for dollars and has tightened the nexus between Congress and K Street, while fueling frustrations about the never-ending monetary arms race to fill campaign coffers.

Some lobbyists who are both big donors and bundlers point out that the fundraising pressures never seems to become nonstop. "It's extraordinarily time consuming for the parties being solicited and those doing the soliciting," says Larry O'Brien, a veteran Democratic lobbyist whose father was the legendary

Lawrence O'Brien of Watergate fame. "As the recipient of these solicitations it's almost exhausting. It's increased dramatically over the last six to eight years."

O'Brien further notes: "Once you've exhausted what you can do as a donor, the next set of calls is to see if you can raise funds. The burden on members is much greater than it used to be." O'Brien points out further that between Tuesday and Thursday of each week, when most D.C. events are organized, "you can probably attend between three and five fundraisers a day. These are breakfasts, lunches, cocktail receptions, and dinners." O'Brien notes that fundraising events outside Washington have also become "ubiquitous," adding further to lobbyists' burdens. Invitations, he quips, have proliferated, with more and more inquiries along the lines of "Do you want to go duck hunting, pheasant hunting, stream fishing, deep-sea fishing, skiing, et cetera?"

Little wonder, then, that many members have become fed up with the current system and are eying further reforms to curb their dependence on lobbyists and special interests for campaign cash. In 2009, bills were introduced in both the House and the Senate that would provide for public funding for congressional candidates.

The House bill, which in early 2010 had garnered 125 co-sponsors, is aimed at reducing the inordinate amounts of time that fundraising now plays in the lives of most members. "It's corrosive to democracy," Rep. John Larson (D-Ct.), a lead sponsor, told me in a phone interview. "It takes away from the amount of time you spend working on issues or with constituents . . . It's always fundraising season. It never stops being fundraising season."

Likewise Rep. Chellie Pingree (D-Maine), who is a sponsor of the public financing bill, is dismayed at the fundraising rat race that members must endure. "Everything in the process is driven by the inordinate amount of money that everyone has to raise to run for office," Pingree said to me. "The whole body is driven by how quickly you can finish the business of the day so you can . . . start raising money."

To lobbyists and big donors, those congressional fundraising demands present a big opening that's often irresistible and easily exploited. "It's natural that members go to people who are looking for access," explains John Jonas, a veteran health-care lobbyist with Patton Boggs, the Democratic-leaning lobbying behemoth. "They're predisposed to give you money and you're giving them something in return. It will be the very strong member who is able to resist those who are generous and regular contributors to them." Jonas adds that it's "very hard to say no to money and not to be appreciative."

Jonas's words certainly ring true in light of the battles waged in 2009 by scores of influence merchants for financial and health-care companies: the two sectors, separately, have plowed hundreds of millions into lobbying and campaign donations to shape and weaken legislation in Congress that would impose new regulations on their businesses. One of the key targets for many financial service lobbyists, for instance, has been the Obama administration proposal to create a new Consumer Financial Products Agency, an idea that most of the big banks and other financial giants detest and that in late 2009 they succeeded in weakening in the version that passed the House.

While the lobbying reform movement in Washington was heating up, the Justice probe of Abramoff's influence-peddling operation chugged along, notching several more convictions, including another high-level Bush administration official.

However, by late 2009, the fact that Ney was the only member who had been convicted puzzled some veteran prosecutors, who voiced a mix of theories about why Justice had not nabbed some of the bigger fish long under scrutiny such as former Reps. DeLay and Doolittle and Ed Buckham.

Some of the harshest criticism leveled at the probe's accomplishments has come from Melanie Sloan of CREW, who faults Justice for a lack of aggressiveness in pursuing both DeLay and Doolittle. "It looks like they were too cautious in indicting people. It's hard to believe you couldn't have gotten an indictment from a grand jury on Doolittle and DeLay. You can show a grand jury that they took things of value in exchange for official action. Public Integrity was way too timid . . . It's a joke that Bob Ney is the highest figure they got."

Not surprisingly, Ney himself seems to agree with Sloan. In his sometimes acerbic comments in the film *Casino Jack*, Ney told Gibrey that after he and Abramoff went to jail, most people assumed that the probe had gone about as far as it could with high-level targets. "What a crock," Ney quipped to Gibney.

Former prosecutors involved in the Abramoff case cite a few factors to explain why the much-publicized probe didn't produce more big-name convictions. Josh Hochberg, who ran the Fraud section for several years, notes that the Abramoff probe wasn't set up with the national resources of the one that Justice mounted a few years before against Enron. "Public corruption investigations are very difficult. Unlike Enron, a team of experienced and seasoned prosecutors was not assembled from around the country with major courtroom experience," Hochberg told me.

Other former Justice lawyers familiar with the Abramoff probe point out that almost from the start of the Justice Department investigation in 2004 there were some serious internal conflicts at Justice about resources and other matters. Among the tensions that seem to have hindered the probe were disagreements—at times quite intense—between the two sections at Justice, Public Integrity and Fraud, working the investigation,

about how hard to press certain cases and whether more resources were needed to ensure that enough experienced hands
were available to bring cases to trial if necessary. "There were
numerous internecine wars among the agents, the prosecutors,
and the hierarchy at Justice, which is never a good thing" says an
ex-prosecutor familiar with the Abramoff case. "At some level
these things always exist. It was well known that the Fraud section wanted to be more aggressive and the Public Integrity section less aggressive."

Despite the internal hassles at Justice and other problems, in
the three years after Abramoff's imprisonment, one high-level
administration official and several Hill aides and Team Abramoff
members were convicted. Arguably the biggest conviction in
these years was the early 2007 plea by Steven Griles, the former
number two at Interior. Griles pleaded guilty to one count of obstruction of justice involving "lying to the Senate about his relationship" with Abramoff. Specifically, Griles acknowledged that
he made false statements in "testimony before the Indian Affairs
Committee in November 2005 and in an earlier interview with
panel investigators."

At Griles' sentencing hearing in June, Judge Ellen Huvelle
again upped the jail time that prosecutors had recommended. In
Griles' case, Huvelle doubled the sentence from the suggested
five months to ten months, citing Griles' apparent failure to understand the seriousness of his misconduct. "Even now you continue to minimize and excuse your conduct," Huvelle told
Griles. In mid-2009, after serving an eight-month jail sentence,
Griles, a once-powerful energy lobbyist prior to the Bush years,
joined a small lobbying and consulting firm.

Not long after the plea by Griles, Italia Federici, the conservative activist who ran the bogus environmental group CREA
and was a key Abramoff ally in efforts to influence decisions by
Interior and Griles, also pled guilty to obstructing a Congres-

sional investigation and tax evasion. Federici, who agreed to cooperate with the probe, in late 2007 received a very mild sentence of two and a half months in a half-way house.

Several other pleas of former Hill aides and Abramoff associates, and especially the trial of Kevin Ring, the aide to Doolittle–turned–Abramoff associate, shed more light on some of the obstacles that Justice faced in pursuing Doolittle.

Of the more recent pleas in 2008 and 2009, a few were at least partly linked to efforts by prosecutors to put more pressure on Ring to plead guilty and provide Justice with more evidence against Doolittle. Ring had cooperated with Justice for almost two years, but he had balked at giving investigators what they most wanted: evidence from Ring that would help make a strong case against Doolittle, in the same way that Neil Volz's evidence had helped convict Ney.

To ratchet up its probes of Ring, who reportedly had a hand in Team Abramoff's hiring of Julie Doolittle (who was paid $96,000 as a consultant), prosecutors brought other corruption charges against several people close to Ring. Among others, separate guilty pleas were entered by Ann Copland, a veteran aide to Sen. Thad Cochran (R. Miss.) who accepted some $25,000 in gifts from Abramoff and his team and helped them with legislative favors; Robert Coughlin, a Justice official who had worked with Ring on the Hill and who was helpful to team Abramoff in securing a much-sought $16 million appropriation for a jail for the Choctaw tribe and received over $4,000 worth of meals and free tickets from Ring; and former Abramoff associate Todd Boulanger, who gave away all expense paid travel and free sports and concert tickets to Hill aides to win legislative help from them.

Not long after these three agreed to plead guilty to separate corruption charges, Justice gave up its efforts to gain Ring's cooperation against Doolittle and indicted him in mid-2009 on eight counts of honest services fraud, one of which involved the hiring of Julie Doolittle. Further, John Doolittle was an unindicted co-conspirator in the case. During Ring's trial in the fall of 2009, his lawyer portrayed many of the charges involving gifts to Hill staffers such as Copland as standard operating procedure for lobbyists and said that they were legal at the time they were given.

Although the defense called no witnesses, Ring's attorney, Andrew Wise, managed to elicit testimony from a few of the prosecution witnesses on cross-examination that made Ring's conduct seem commonplace. In a closing argument to the jury, Ring's attorney said, "It sounds sinister to talk about meals and tickets, near in time to when folks are being asked to take official actions," but he added that "it is the way that politics works. This is not the sign of a bribe. This is not the sign of a corrupt relationship."

Ultimately, the government's case failed to convince the jurors, and after several days of deliberation, the judge declared a mistrial. Ring's attorneys then argued successfully to put off a second trial until after June 2010, when the Supreme Court would hand down a ruling on three separate cases involving the honest services fraud statute, a decision that could have a sizable impact on the case against Ring. (The statute, which was one of the charges against Abramoff and Ney, has become a favorite of prosecutors in recent years because it is vaguer than the traditional bribery statutes and doesn't require that there be an explicit quid pro quo. Instead, fraud charges can be brought against a politician or lobbyist for failing to fulfill their obligations to their constituents or clients respectively. Based on a number of tough questions that several Supreme Court Justices asked last fall in hearing two cases involving private honest services fraud and one involving public honest services fraud, many legal analysts expect the court to sharply curb the use of the statutes and set stricter guidelines for their usage.)

Despite—and perhaps also because of—the length of the Abramoff probe and the intense press coverage it spawned, the public has received an eye-opening education in just how much lobbyists now shape legislative and regulatory battles on a myriad of fronts from health care to financial services. Meanwhile, public awareness about influence-peddling in Washington policy matters seemed to expand with the media coverage of the hugely expensive lobbying battles in 2009 over health care, financial services, and climate-change legislation. Each of these mega-fights entailed new regulations that sparked strong lobbying opposition from health care, finance, and energy interests and, combined, involved the expenditure of hundreds of millions of dollars in lobbying and campaign contributions to weaken or defeat the various bills.

Even as the Abramoff scandal faded from the national headlines at the start of the Obama administration, it was obvious that the spotlight on lobbying had intensified and sparked more public cynicism.

Notwithstanding the manifest ways that Abramoff trampled laws and norms in Washington, he also left a legacy as a model fundraiser and bundler extraordinaire that became part of the wider lobbying culture: during and since his salad days on K Street, dozens of other Republican and Democratic lobbyists have assumed major tasks as money bundlers for presidential campaigns, as well as for leadership PACs and ordinary House and Senate races.

Even Senator John McCain, in his 2008 presidential drive, turned to numerous prominent lobbyists on K Street for their crucial help as big-time money bundlers, much as President Bush had done in his two campaigns. In late 2008, Justice turned its sights on another potentially explosive lobbying scandal involving the PMA Group, a now-defunct, largely Democratic lobbying firm, which was legendary for helping its defense clients win tens of millions in earmarks from House appropriators, several of whom serendipitously benefitted from hundreds of thousands in campaign contributions from the clients and the PMA lobbyists.

These fundraising bonds, which the lobbying community thrives on for its access and influence, are viewed by many watchdog groups and members as the most pernicious part of the prevailing K Street culture and what needs to be fixed above all else. To many, Abramoff's lobbying operation was indicative of the way that Washington increasingly has become dominated by special-interest money and lobbying. Melanie Sloan of CREW, for instance, finds much in the Abramoff story that serves as a microcosm of how Washington works, "A lot of Abramoff's actions were just the way the game is played in Washington now."

The way that the game is played has certainly led to a financial bonanza for the lobbying business, says Rep. Pingree, and it isn't pretty. Ultimately, she concludes, "A whole group of people have access and influence because you need them to write a check."

Sources

This book grew out of reporting over a two-year period that started in the spring of 2004. It began with a six-page profile of Abramoff that I wrote for *National Journal*, where I have covered lobbying and money and politics issues since 1992. Following the profile, I reported regularly on the scandal as it evolved for *National Journal*, while researching and writing the book during the latter half of 2005 and early 2006.

My reporting has been enriched by interviews with some fifty former lobbying colleagues, conservative activists, old friends of Abramoff's, and his onetime associate Michael Scanlon and others, who spoke to me mostly on background and wanted to remain anonymous in large part because of the criminal probe under way at Justice. I interviewed some people many times and am grateful for their patience and help over many months, as I tried to dig deeper into different parts of the scandal and Abramoff's decade-long lobbying career in Washington, plus his quarter century of ties to the conservative movement.

The public hearings that the Senate Committee on Indian Affairs held in 2004 and 2005 into how Abramoff and Scanlon bilked six casino-rich tribes out of $82 million over a three-year period were an invaluable source of material for me, as they were for many other reporters covering the scandal. In particular, the thousands of e-mails and other documents that the panel released were a rich source of anecdotes, quotes, leads, and revealing insights into the frauds committed by Abramoff and Scanlon.

In the course of my reporting, I visited three of the tribes—the Tiguas in El Paso, Texas; the Saginaw Chippewas in Mount Pleasant, Michigan; and the Louisiana Coushattas in Kinder, Louisiana—where I spent several days interviewing tribal leaders and others who had dealings with Abramoff and Scanlon.

I interviewed Abramoff on the phone in late March 2004 for *National Journal*, but he declined to talk to me for the book, although I made several requests through his spokesman, Andrew Blum. Abramoff also declined to answer a two-page list of written questions that I submitted as I was finishing the book. Scanlon too refused requests to be interviewed for the book.

My research into Abramoff and the lobbying scandal benefited considerably from the work of several other reporters who were covering the story. No one reporting on the scandal can match the work that was done by Susan Schmidt and her two colleagues, James Grimaldi and R. Jeffrey Smith, at *The Washington Post*, who joined her in helping to unravel one of the biggest public corruption tales in decades. They richly deserved the Pulitzer Prize for investigative reporting that they won in 2006. Several other reporters provided first-rate coverage of parts of the scandal. They include John Bresnahan of *Roll Call*; Michael Crowley and Franklin Foer of *The New Republic*; Glen Justice, Anne Kornblut, and Philip Shenon of *The New York Times*; Chuck Neubauer, Walter Roche, and Richard Schmitt of the *Los Angeles Times*; Michael Kranish of *The Boston Globe*; Jim Galloway of *The Atlanta Journal-Constitution*; Karen Tumulty and Massimo Calabrese of *Time*; and Jeanne Cummings and Brody Mullins of *The Wall Street Journal*.

The following articles and books were particularly helpful in researching and writing the book.

MAGAZINE AND NEWSPAPER ARTICLES

John Cassidy, "The Ringleader," *The New Yorker*, August 1, 2005.

Nicholas Confessore, "Welcome to the Machine," *Washington Monthly*, July/August 2003.

Matthew Continetti, "Money, Mobsters, Murder," *The Weekly Standard*, November 28, 2005.

Michael Crowley, "A Lobbyist in Full," *The New York Times Magazine*, May 1, 2005.

Elizabeth Drew, "Selling Washington," *The New York Review of Books*, June 23, 2005.

Andrew Ferguson, "A Lobbyist's Progress," *The Weekly Standard*, December 20, 2004.

David Margolick, "Washington's Invisible Man," *Vanity Fair*, April 2006.

Julia Robb, "Millions Misspent?," *The Town Talk*, September 21, 2003.

Susan Schmidt and James V. Grimaldi, "Untangling a Lobbyist's Stake in Casino Fleet," *The Washington Post*, May 1, 2005.

R. Jeffrey Smith, "The DeLay-Abramoff Money Trail," *The Washington Post*, December 31, 2005.

Barry Yeoman, "The Fall of a True Believer," *Mother Jones*, September/October 2005.

BOOKS

Elizabeth Drew, *Whatever It Takes: The Real Struggle for Political Power in America* (New York: Viking, 1997).

Lou Dubose and Jan Reid, *The Hammer: Tom DeLay, God, Money, and the Rise of the Republican Congress* (New York: Public Affairs, 2004).

Nina J. Easton, *Gang of Five: Leaders at the Center of the Conservative Crusade* (New York: Simon & Schuster, 2000).

David Maraniss and Michael Weisskopf, *"Tell Newt to Shut Up!"* (New York: Simon & Schuster, 1996).

U.S. Senate, Committee on Indian Affairs, *Tribal Lobbying Matters*, 4 vols. September 29, 2004; June 22, November 2, November 17, 2005 (Washington, D.C.: GPO, 2005), www.gpo.gov.

Acknowledgements

A book about a political scandal that is constantly shifting and evolving has to be something of a roller-coaster experience, and this one was no exception. It couldn't have been written without the generous encouragement of friends, journalistic colleagues, my publisher, and my family.

From the start of this project in the spring of 2005, my editors at *National Journal*—especially the magazine's editor, Charlie Green, and managing editor, Bob Gettlin—have been exceedingly supportive and understanding of the time pressures that I faced. A few longtime magazine colleagues and one alum—James Barnes, Richard Cohen, and Dick Kirschten—were kind enough to read large parts of the book in both its earlier and more polished stages, and offered much appreciated and sage advice. Two younger colleagues, Peter Bell and Gregg Sangillo, did yeoman's service in fact-checking.

At Farrar, Straus and Giroux, I owe a huge debt to my terrific editor, Eric Chinski, who first approached me in late 2004 when the scandal was still unfolding about whether there was a book to be done on Abramoff, his conservative allies, and the bilking of the several casino-rich Indian tribes. During my research and writing, Eric was a constant source of encouragement, good humor, and, most important, excellent editing ideas. Many smaller details along the way were handled with grace by Gena Ham-shaw, Eric's very capable assistant. Jeff Seroy, FSG's first-rate publicity director, was a pleasure to work with too.

Finally, I owe a big thanks to my very special and loving family for putting up with my often obsessive interest in the scandal for more than a year. First my cousins, aunt, and uncle in the Stone clan of writers—Chris Stone, Celia Gilbert, Judy Stone, and Lou Stone—were very helpful, listening to my war stories and complaints and providing lots of inspiration. My wife, Eve Ottenberg, an accomplished book reviewer and novelist, ably critiqued large parts of the book, and our three children, Nicholas, Madeleine, and Jasmine, were all wonderful: they deserve the publishing equivalent of Olympic gold medals for keeping me on track and laughing during some of the tougher moments in finishing this book.

A Note on the Paperback

In the course of working on the paperback, I also served as a consultant on the documentary Casino Jack by Academy Award-winner Alex Gibney, a role that included providing help in lining up several Abramoff associates and acquaintances who appear in the film. While my cover is graced with the film's poster art and uses the film's title, the paperback is distinct from, and in no way based on, Gibney's fine documentary, although several telling quotes in this revised edition are taken from the film. Likewise, Gibney's film is not based on what was originally published as Heist or the paperback edition. We are each responsible for the themes and contents of our works.

I also owe a special thanks to Kelly Burdick, my editor at Melville House, who encouraged this new, updated and expanded paperback edition. And I'd also like to acknowledge my gratitude to veteran investigative reporter and editor, Ed Pound, a former colleague at National Journal, who graciously offered to lend his deft editorial touch to help strengthen the epilogue.

Index